The Boy from the Wild

PETER MEYER

WITH

GRAHAM SPENCE

This book is dedicated to my wonderful father

Email: book@petermeyer.com

Website: www.petermeyer.com

Facebook: @theboyfromthewild

Social Media Accounts for Acting: @petermeyeractor

Prologue

JAMES MEYER STOOD ON TOP of a wild, windswept peak, overlooking the valley that opened up below as far as the eye could see.

In the haze of morning sunlight burning off cloud, it shimmered like a verdant mirage, stretching east until it butted against a cluster of kopjes on the horizon. Lush bushveld peppered with mist-belt forests glistened in a kaleidoscope of greens ranging from jade to dark emerald. The hills, including the peak James was standing on, towered above like the citadels of Shangri-La, guarding secret treasures.

James stood as still as a gecko as he absorbed the spectacle. It was Biblical in its magnificence. It was Paradise.

A river flowed deep in the valley. He could see where it came tumbling out of the hills in an exuberant torrent, one of several waterfalls as it flowed with restless energy towards the Indian Ocean.

The valley was called Karkloof, named after the river below that had carved its course through the fertile lands millennia ago. The Zulus called it The Valley of Heaven...which was as succinct as one could get.

James breathed deeply, inhaling this vision of Eden. He was 16, a pupil at Hilton College, a boys-only boarding school near the town of Hilton in the KwaZulu-Natal Midlands of South Africa. The northern section of the school estate was a proclaimed nature reserve and pupils would spend Sundays hiking, swimming, tubing down rivers, mountain biking, fishing, bird watching and exploring the wild. The school considered that an important part of a youth's education, but only for those who understood the spirituality of wild places.

James understood. Something primal shifted in his core. He knew something pivotal had happened. This was where he would be one day.

James was a born adventurer. He loved the outdoors; the wilderness. He loved excitement. Although born and bred in England, it did not take long for Africa to capture his soul.

Blond, muscular with Hollywood good looks, James could charm his way in or out of anything. He wanted to be an explorer — to live a life of action and quest. On his holidays he would head to the beaches of Durban, which at the time was the Malibu of the southern hemisphere, and surf the biggest and wildest waves he could. Even the regular shark scares in those days before nets were installed did not deter him. In fact, they added spice.

With his ready smile, his charisma and easy manner, he was impossible not to like. His friends gathered around knowing they were in for some fun. Girls found him irresistible.

"C'mon James. Let's go tubing down the river." It was his best friend, Deneys Hattingh, grabbing James's arm to get him moving.

Deneys, like James, was a youthful swashbuckler. He was the archetypical friend that you treasure, but don't particularly want to introduce to your parents. Deneys was a rebel, and found in James a kindred spirit. He too loved the bush, surfing and girls.

"Wait a minute."

Deneys followed James gaze across the valley. He let go James's arm and put his hand to his forehead, squinting against the sun.

"Pretty impressive, huh?"

James nodded. He silently made a vow. One day he would come back to this valley. One day he would own it. He would make it into one of the most spectacular game reserves in Africa.

James took his vows seriously, but a lot got in the way after that fateful day.

He had plenty of living to do, and James characteristically grabbed life with both hands.

He was one of the first people to drive from Cairo to Cape Town, crossing the Sahara on barely visible tracks, and then returned to England to run the family property development business.

The company was already a pioneer in the burgeoning real estate industry, building the first shopping malls in England. James turned the business from big to massive, becoming a multi-millionaire before he turned 30.

But he never forgot that pledge to own a stretch of paradise in Africa.

I am his eldest blood son. That vow he made has defined my life.

Chapter 1

Running wild

I WAS BORN IN AFRICA, the first of our English paternal line to draw his opening gasp on the wild continent.

My mother, however, was South African, so Africa was already wired into my DNA.

My father even chose my birthplace, Durban, as it was a city he loved and also one of the glamour metropolises of the day. At the time, my parents were living in the Limpopo Province in the far north-east of South Africa, but Durban was special to my dad. He had spent his formative years there and loved the carefree attitude, the long, flat waterfront with its world class beaches, the salty tang of spray from Indian

Ocean waves that cleansed the air and the exotic aromas ranging from tropical fruit to spicy Indian curries.

But I knew little of the endless summer beaches and surfing that my dad experienced while growing up. My home was the bush. My earliest memories are the freedom of the wild and of life being one glorious adventure. Other children may fantasise about running feral, but we at Karkloof Nature Reserve were doing it every day. We took it for granted. In fact, we didn't know any different. We were living the dream without actually knowing what the dream was.

It's only now, nearly three decades later, that I realise what a privileged, carefree life I had. My home today skirts the concrete jungle of London and is a galaxy removed from the genuine jungles of my childhood. I live a few miles off one of Europe's busiest motorways, the insanely congested M25 that circles London like an engorged python. In Karkloof, our roads were often little more than tracks. The main traffic was Land Rovers and the only congestion was herds of wild animals crossing to fresh pastures.

The bush was our back garden, overlooking the valley of heaven surrounded by savannah, riverbanks, rugged cliff edges, kopjes and woodland. It was unlike any garden that most children could ever imagine. Cicadas hummed the soothing buzz of Africa and the exuberant bird life chirped incessantly, roosting in trees or soaring like sultans in the skies. Red-winged francolins sang and trumpeter hornbills squawked plaintive cries, while nesting fish eagles yelped tunes only heard in Africa. Circling above, you often would see crowned eagles or forest buzzards, while perched in branches overhanging the river malachite kingfishers hunted tilapia, spearing the fish with surgical precision.

Unlike a tame garden with manicured lawns and arranged flowers, playing in the wild meant that you never knew what lurked around the corner. Or just as ominously, what was slithering under a rock. We had forests and savannah and watering holes all around us. We spent our days catching, or trying to catch, snakes, scorpions, lizards, spiders — even baby leguaans if their mothers weren't around. For me it was normal at the time. I thought it was what all kids did.

Other games we played were daring each other to see who could get closest to a rhino before it spun around, nimble as a matador despite its massive bulk. Sometimes we threw stones at them, trying to get their attention, knowing that all a stone could do to these magnificent iron-skinned creatures was irritate them. Which it certainly did.

We were having amazing adventures before I was even six years-old. On one occasion I tossed a stone which struck a rhino squarely on its rump. Faster than an eye could blink, it had swivelled and was coming for me. You cannot believe how quick these seemingly ungainly juggernauts are.

I fled, pumping my little legs as fast as I could. It was no contest and panic-stricken I looked for a tree to climb.

There were none close enough. But fortunately, just a few yards ahead, the ground sloped steeply. I plunged down the incline knowing that the two-ton beast would not follow me. A rhino is too bulky to defy gravity in a sprint downhill, so I was safe.

This was our version of playing chicken, the bush version of PlayStation. Except it was no game. The rhino coming for me was not digitally created by some Silicon Valley computer geek; this was 2,000 kilograms of stomping muscle with a scimitar at one end. The stakes were far higher than we imagined. Suffice it to say that I was instantly cured of willingly tempting fate with these behemoths ever again.

I never told my parents about that charge as I would have been confined indoors. Or at the very least, not allowed to roam the reserve without a ranger nearby. To me, there was no greater punishment. Even at that young age, I knew there were certain stories that my mother would rather not hear. My father would have been even more livid, not just because of the danger, but it was being contemptuous to animals, something he could not tolerate. I agree with him completely. We were not only being stupid, but disrespectful.

Another time I nearly got into trouble was when I was about five years old and had to do homework, which was purgatory for a boy who lived for the bush. My mum was adamant that I could not go outside until my assignment was finished.

I was so angry that I threatened to run away and live with my grandmother in England. Mum said okay and even packed me a small lunch box.

I stormed out of the house and started walking to the airport. I had no idea where the airport was, or that I needed a passport to get a plane ticket. I just knew that a world which demanded that boys like me do homework was not worth living in.

I walked for more than two miles and when I rounded a bend I came face to face with a herd of wildebeest. A wildebeest is an African gnu with a shaggy head and short, sharp horns. They are not normally dangerous, but if they feel threatened, they will sometimes charge you. Particularly a small boy. They have been known to kill people, on very rare occasions.

But what was far more ominous was that I could see buffalo in the distance. Now those are extremely dangerous. And they were getting closer.

I wasn't scared as I was still so incensed at being 'jailed' indoors. But I was a little apprehensive — even more so as the browsing buffalo kept shifting closer. Buffalos gather in herds. This was not like creeping up on some solitary rhino.

Suddenly my mum arrived, flung open the door and told me to get into the car. She had been following slowly from a distance. When she saw the buffalo, she put her foot on the accelerator to get me out of harm's way as quickly as possible.

I jumped into the car with all thoughts of running off to England disappearing into the ether.

I still finished my packed lunch. But at home, rather than at the airport.

As we grew older, we became more 'creative' in our escapades. My cousin Guy-Guy (so named to differentiate from his uncle called Guy) and I would walk around the picnic areas where tourists gathered and we'd tell them our 'mummy hasn't fed us' and we were hungry. Did they have any money to spare?

Amazingly, many people fell for it despite the fact that we were wearing Karkloof Reserve uniforms — khakis with epaulets — and it was blatantly evident that we were not starving. Also people coming to the game reserve, which was obviously doing very well judging by the volume of tourists, must have wondered why the owner's son was begging for money.

Anyway, we were very successful and would go and buy ice cream and sweets at the reserve's amusement centre with our ill-gotten gains.

Then somebody told my parents. To say they were appalled is the understatement of the year. We were banished in disgrace back to the lodge.

On another occasion an important client who had driven up from Durban for a meeting with my dad arrived in his fancy car, which he parked outside the main lodge. For some reason — I still have no idea why — Guy and I thought it would be fun to hide it under a pile of rocks.

The vehicle in question was a brand new, top of the range BMW and we had almost completed the job when my dad and the client came out.

"What are you doing?" he roared.

"Er … hiding this car."

"Take those rocks away."

Unfortunately, we had scratched some of the glistening metal work, which was not appreciated by the owner.

After that expensive prank, my parents decided that Guy-Guy and I were bad influences on each other and separated us.

Guy-Guy was great fun, although as naughty as all hell, but my greatest childhood friend was a Zulu boy called Pugga, whose mother worked at the lodge. The big adventure for us kids was going out on picnics on our own. We knew of the dangers and limits of what lurked in the veld, but we were just kids and exploring. Life was one big adventure. We wanted to know where the river went; what was in the cave up in the hills. We were exploring new ground every day — just going and seeing stuff and not worrying about anything.

The lessons we were learning were far removed from children of my age in the cities. Kids there are taught to look left and right for on-coming traffic. Pugga and I had to look everywhere for animals, and what to do to avoid them. We also learned what plants were poisonous, not to walk near cliff edges, or where the currents in a river were too wild.

Our expeditions were not ordinary children's outings. We'd pack our food in a rucksack, gather our animal-hide shields and small assegais — Zulu spears — then hike three or four miles to a waterfall on the Karkloof River. There we would set up camp between huge boulders smoothed by centuries of river flow and pretend we were real men of the wild, climbing trees and jumping into the plunge pool beneath the falls.

There were two falls on the reserve, the larger being the famous Karkloof Falls, which at 98 metres is one of the highest waterfalls in South Africa. To get there and back involved an all-day trek through dense bush and against the flow of the river.

The second waterfall was closer and smaller, although still pretty big, and that was our favourite place. The prime spot was a rocky ledge behind the falls where we could stand and have a spray-shower from heaven.

We had to be careful though, as the pools below the falls were also watering holes for animals. So whenever we heard a strange sound we would hide in case a rhino or buffalo herd was coming down for a drink.

However, the most fun was a zipline tied to a high riverbank tree on the other side of the valley near the reserve's campsite. It was a helter-skelter ride across the river and you could either drop off into the plunge pool, or if you kept going you would land in bulrushes lining the bank. It was pretty steep; you didn't want to fall off the zipline too soon, but you also needed serious *cojones* to keep going and land on the far bank as the reeds grew in gooey mud that gripped like quicksand.

One of my more memorable 'zooms' down the zipline was speeding all the way into the bulrushes and crashing into a giant leguaan. The word leguaan is an Afrikaans corruption of the word iguana. Non-Africans would call it a monitor lizard and it's a cousin of the komodo dragon with a temperament to match. Our faces were inches apart, and we both reared back in shock. I can still picture it clearly, the reptile's pink mouth gaping open and it let out a harsh angry rasp that sounded like something between a hiss and a growl. Then it ran straight over me.

It was huge, the size of a juvenile crocodile. We knew it was there as we often saw it sunning itself on the rocks. But I never thought I would bang straight into it while zip-lining.

I had been attacked by a leguaan before and have a healthy respect for them. Once one came into the restaurant on the reserve and I stupidly tried to catch it by grabbing it from behind. Quick as a blink it lashed out with its tail, whipping it around my leg. It was excruciatingly painful — like being flicked hard with a wet towel, or stung by a swarm of wasps. Luckily, it was a small one.

These wonderful river expeditions with Pugga became the bedrock of my bush education. Our mothers packed picnic lunches, sandwiches for me, while Pugga had *pap* —a stiff maize meal porridge that we ate with our fingers. I preferred the Zulu food to the sandwiches, and Pugga was always very generous, as best friends should be.

Our mothers worried about us going off alone and we were warned with dire threats of serious punishment to stay on the footpaths and not go running into the bush. Of course we ignored that. This meant regularly coming face to face with rhinos or buffaloes and having to back off slowly, often waiting for several hours for the animals to move away. Then we would be home late and lie to our parents saying we had unwittingly gone further upriver than we intended. Any mention of being treed by a rhino or buffalo would have resulted in our picnics being instantly banned. Of that there is no doubt.

Strangely, our hairiest moment together was not from a rhino or buffalo, but from a wildebeest. We were walking along an animal path lined with long grass and suddenly there in front of me was a baby wildebeest. It stood still, just looking at me. At first I thought it was injured. Pugga was about 30 paces behind, looking for stones to use as sinkers for our fishing lines.

I signalled him to stop. We didn't move, keeping calm and quiet when suddenly the mother burst out of the thicket.

To be between a mother and baby is the worst possible scenario in the bush. Globally, more people are killed by mothers protecting their young than any other wilderness accident. In such situations you either hold your ground if the animal is motionless, but if it charges, you lie flat to show you are no threat.

The worst thing to do is run as that provokes a charge, rather like a dog chasing a cat. But Pugga was not going to waste time considering options. Just behind him was a large freestanding acacia that we regularly climbed to escape animals. He was up the flat-topped tree faster than a leopard.

I was too far away to reach the acacia in time, so I flung myself down and hugged the ground. The wildebeest sped straight past, its pounding hooves inches from my head. I was very lucky not to get stomped.

Fortunately, as soon as the wildebeest reached its baby, it nudged the youngster off into the bush away from me to join the rest of the herd.

"Hey, Pugga," I shouted, laughing in sheer relief as he climbed down the tree looking a little sheepish. "Thanks for all the support."

To us, this was just another adventure. We were as close as brothers. He always had my back, just as I had his. I think that was one of the main reasons our parents trusted us together in the bush

Sometimes my younger brother Jamie and a boy from the neighbouring farm, Brent Leo-Smith joined us. Brent was hardcore, even at that young age. When Pugga and I came across tourists, we would pretend to impress them by sticking a finger into rhino or buffalo scat, then licking it and sagely opining that it was 'fresh'. The animals were here 'about an hour ago' we'd inform them, nodding like wise men of the wild. Of course, we wouldn't lick the actual finger we had stuck into the poo, but the tourists wouldn't know that.

Brent, however, went all the way. He would lick his poo-smeared finger with relish, enjoying the look of horror on the tourists' faces.

That was his idea of a practical joke, but one we played on him was far funnier. He was sleeping after a picnic by the pool and Pugga and I tied his bootlaces together. It was a situation we could not resist, because Brent seldom wore boots. As I said, he was hardcore and his idea of footwear was his bare feet, which seemed impervious to thorns that grew like weeds in the bush.

I then shouted, "Look out! Rhino!" and Brent leapt up, falling flat on his face as he tried to sprint off. He made several panic-stricken attempts to get up until he saw us collapsed with laughter.

Brent also had the 'bright' idea of starting a fire by concentrating sunrays on dry grass with a magnifying glass, something we had learned at school. We were no strangers to fires as many meals in Africa are cooked over coals. It's called a 'braai', the local word for barbecue. We also regularly burned grassland to rejuvenate grazing for animals, but these fires were all strictly controlled.

However, we had never actually started a veld fire ourselves. It was a blistering hot day. We collected a pile of twigs and brown grass and using the magnifying glass, had it smoking in no time.

Suddenly it flared up. We had no water, so Brent and I started peeing on the flames now rapidly leaping out of control while Pugga desperately shovelled sand onto the heart of the blaze, trying to smother it. Fortunately, it didn't spread, but Les Carlisle, our head ranger, heard about it and gave me a hiding and a stern talking to. We never tried that stunt again.

Apart from putting fingers in poo and peeing on fires, Brent's other claim to fame was that his mother is the highest-ever ranked South African women's tennis player, winning the Wimbledon mixed doubles in 1977 and 1980. Her maiden name was Greer Stevens and she is still a legend in sporting circles. Brent later also became well-known in his own right as a wildlife photographer for National Geographic. It was our reserve at Karkloof that nurtured his love of the wilderness and wildlife.

Pugga left us a couple of years later when his mother took another job. Sadly, I have no idea where he is today or how to contact him or his family. I don't even know if he is still alive. But I will never forget him.

I was six years old and growing up fast. Not in a sophisticated sense, but in understanding the natural world. I was a child of the bush; a child of Africa.

And there was no better role model than my father.

Chapter 2

Dad

THE MEYER AFRICAN ODYSSESY did not start off on a particularly positive note. The short version is that my father's family came to the continent primarily because my grandfather had serious respiratory problems.

He was diagnosed in England and told by his doctor that a possible cure was to live in a hot, humid climate. At the very least, it would ease his breathing difficulties. England may be many things, but it is certainly neither hot nor humid.

The choice was California, or Durban in South Africa. So he, his wife and four children set sail for a new life 6,000 miles away.

Another reason, as I have just learned from my dad's revered private assistant Paddy Fink, was that the Second World War had broken out and the British army was on the run at Dunkirk. As my grandfather was Jewish, he had grave concerns for his family if Britain lost the war — which seemed extremely likely in those bleak early days. He wanted to settle in a neutral country, and South Africa seemed to be the better bet with both climate and security.

Several years later my father James was sent to school at Hilton College. It didn't take long for the wilderness bug to bite him, nurtured by the fact that although Hilton was an exclusive private school, it was also way out in the bush.

However, he had the best of both worlds as in those days Durban was the Malibu of the southern hemisphere as well as the wave riding hub of Africa. He was living the good life; surfing, sun, sea and sand…and plenty of bikini-clad girls.

A lot of people have remarked that he was the James Dean of his time. The fact that he was the spitting image of actor Patrick Swayze — and also danced like him — no doubt helped.

His best friend, both on the beach and at school, was Deneys Hattingh, with whom he shared many adventures.

Deneys, now in his late 70s, remembers those halcyon years well.

"During our holidays we spent most of our time on South Beach in Durban, attracted by the sun, the waves and the fairer sex. These were carefree days filled with fun and parties. It coincided with the start of the surfing craze, although surfing then was nothing like it is today. We had to make our own boards, big, bulky, clumsy affairs that had minds of their own. I can recall yelling and shouting to warn unsuspecting bathers to get out of the way of our erratic approach!"

After leaving school, Deneys and James continued hanging out together, determined to live life to the full. Their next adventure was a trip to Zimbabwe, which was called Rhodesia at the time.

In typical fashion, they turned the 1,044-mile trip into a Le Mans race track, doing it in under 19 hours and breaking the unofficial record. Although that may not sound particularly impressive by today's standards, one has to remember that many of the roads were either rickety tar strips, or even worse, rutted dirt tracks.

"These hazards were negotiated at speeds in excess of 80 mph, which was not recommended," said Deneys.

In other words, this was extreme rally driving before the sport became fashionable. Flimsy roads, potholes as deep as dongas and fallen branches blocking the way were not the only hazards. Nor the most dangerous.

"One incident worth relating was running into a black mamba which reared up in front of us," recalled Deneys. "As we struck it, the snake whiplashed into the back of our open car. Both of us leapt out while the vehicle was still running. Despite a cautious search we never found the snake — thank God!"

That was what Dad loved most; fast cars, action, wild escapades and living on the edge. An aura of excitement cloaked him wherever he went. Things happened when Jimmy Meyer was around. As a result, people relished being with him, charmed like metal to a magnet.

When his mother and father left Durban, returning to England to resume running the family property business, Dad opted to stay behind. He had no interest in leaving Africa. He was having too much fun.

Not long afterwards he got an urgent message from his father; please come home.

Again he refused. Why would he return to the cold northern high latitudes?

Then he learned the truth. His dad was dying of stomach cancer. It was spreading fast and was terminal. Jimmy was needed back in England to take over Ideal Homes, the family business. It was a residential property company that was doing extremely well. In fact, my grandfather had been one of the pioneers of council housing that provided affordable accommodation for millions of Britons.

With a heavy heart, Dad waved goodbye to his many friends in Africa and returned to the grey clouds of Surrey. The carefree, Bohemian days of sun-drenched beaches, girls and sports cars would have to wait while he steered the multi-million-pound family venture through turbulent times.

However, he had one condition. He would only come back if his best friend Deneys Hattingh accompanied him. I think that although my father knew the serious side of his life had now started, he still wanted to keep the fun part alive. That's why he wanted Deneys to join the business. Deneys was the guy he always got into trouble with; the guy with whom he chased girls and rode big waves off Durban's coast. He was a good guy to have on your side.

My grandfather died soon afterwards, leaving my dad solely in charge of the property empire. Dad had no experience in running a multi-million-pound enterprise, so he had to learn fast. This was when many people first realised what a remarkable person he was.

Dad had little time to grieve, but he did so deeply. Even more than he ever realised as he felt guilty that for much of his life he had never got on well with his father.

The big difference was their opposing temperaments. My father was a fiercely independent man while grandad was far more traditional. He was a big businessman and did things conventionally, which completely contrasted to my dad's flamboyance. It was a clash of two exceptionally strong characters.

Only at the end did my father realize how much he loved his own father. How much he would desperately miss him. Many years later he told me that one of the few regrets of his own eventful life was that he had not spent more time with his father. He said he had never properly thanked him for the amazing privileges bestowed on him. He bitterly regretted that for the rest of his life. Thankfully, they did bond in the final months, but my father wished that he had realized earlier what an incredible person his own father had been.

My grandfather's death changed everything. Overnight, my dad's dream of a game ranch in Africa, his vision of the Valley of Heaven that emerged as an ethereal mirage below the soaring cliffs, was now on the backburner. He had a business to run so he did it the only way he knew — at full throttle. He went to night school to learn the intricacies of financial management and ran the company during the day. It was a crash course of harsh business realities forged in the rough-and-tumble corporate jungle mixed with cold classroom theory in the evening. He excelled at both.

Dad did everything with total commitment. My grandfather had been the initial visionary but it was my father who took the business to soaring new heights. He then started his own property company, Federated Homes, as well as a separate commercial property development company called Federated Developments, and was the youngest person ever to get a million-pound loan from Barclays — in the days of real money and tight-fisted bankers.

My dad had two goals; to make his company one of the best in the world, and more importantly, to make his father proud of him, even though the old man was no longer alive. He had inherited an impressive legacy from a man he loved deeply, but he had been too headstrong to admit it. He was not going to squander that.

Deneys was at his side during that harsh baptism of High Street fire. They also had loads of laughs along the way.

"The company, with James now at the helm, bought a block of land and buildings in Cheam, south east of London," said Deneys. "Included in the deal were a number of going concerns which included a pub, some minor shops and a motor business. We tossed a coin to see who would manage which activities, and guess what? James got the pub while I got the motor business.

"However, the lack of car sales required many brainstorming sessions in the pub which usually ended with an abundance of solutions but no effective conclusions."

Dad soon showed what a business genius he was, turning run-of-the-mill deals into profitable ventures.

"A block of 66 flats was later built on that land and sold," said Deneys, noting with some sadness that the pub where all the brainstorming had occurred was demolished in the process. "The development company was now on its way.

James had the Midas touch and an incredible knack of spotting a good thing. The company went from strength to strength, finally ending up building and selling some 1,350 homes a year. This took hard work and James was not deterred. His impressive work ethic was infectious and success was built upon success."

Dad then opened up a construction company which, under his guidance, was also a winner.

Deneys remembers one of their more spectacular deals.

"James purchased a large tract of land with a lake in the middle, which for most people would pose a problem. Not for James. Next to the land was a golf course and after a good deal of negotiation we sold the lake to the golf club. In reality, all this entailed was digging a hole on the golf course and draining the lake into it, which we did."

However, the construction workers needed to know the depth of the lake, so Dad summoned his lead Contracts Manager, Ted Allen to measure it.

Ted arrived in a Saville Row suit and shiny leather shoes, unaware that he would have to row out in a small rubber dinghy with a lead weight tied to a length of string.

He gamely got into the tiny boat, still in his expensive suit, and started rowing.

Unfortunately, as he got to the middle, the dinghy's air-valve popped out and the boat started to sink.

Ted started to panic, understandably not wanting to get his top of the range clothes wet. When he realised that he had no chance of reaching shore in time, he stood up with an 'oh shit' look on his face, and like a good captain went down with his ship.

This was prime front row entertainment for the construction crew on the bank. One worker came up to my dad and said, "Okay, at least we know it's deeper than 6 feet."

Ted was 6'1", and that was the measurement used for digging the new lake. My dad was rolling on the ground he was laughing so much.

Still, it was a win-win situation, although maybe not for the surveyor. The golfers were ecstatic with their new water feature, while Dad were even happier with the additional 66 apartments that his company built on the reclaimed land.

He then constructed the first shopping centres in the U.K, but even though he was always thinking big, he kept the human touch. He had a passionate 'feel' for the industry. For example, one property he built in Dorking outside London is now, many years later, the Head Office for the travel company Kuoni Holidays. When Dad was developing the site, he discovered a Second World War bomb shelter, and instead of bulldozing it down, he incorporated it into the architectural design. Many years later when I was working in Jamaica and on a business trip to the U.K, I took my sales team to the building, as Kuoni was one of our travel partners. When I told them my dad had built it and showed them the bunker, they were stunned at how a major property developer had gone out of his way to preserve a piece of history that would otherwise have been destroyed. In fact, office staff in the building had no idea why the old bunker was there in a modern building, and were fascinated when I explained its history. They certainly have far more respect for their offices today.

Federated was fast becoming the largest and most successful property development company in the U.K, and Dad was hailed as one of Britain's top businessmen. The company employed more than 1,000 staff and was the go-to real estate group in both the U.K and, increasingly, Europe. He also built shopping centres and golf courses in America, using concepts pioneered in England and making them bigger and better in the States

From being the James Dean of the surfing set in Durban, he was now the James Dean of the London business world. He also acquired the 'toys' that came with being a star businessman, his particular favourites being a helicopter and a string of show jumping horses. The helicopter was practical — Jimmy had so many meetings to attend that it was easier to fly in. But his passion was horse riding.

Most mornings would find him galloping at breakneck speed across the Surrey heaths, re-charging his batteries in the brisk, misty English dawns in preparation for the hectic day ahead. He was a superb horseman, competing and beating professionals at top events, including Hickstead, Wimbledon and Badminton.

The Stable Manager of Dad's horse yard was Carolyn Boyd, who was also destined to play a pivotal role in the fortunes of the Meyer family.

"It was 1978 when I applied for a position as Stable Manager to run his show jumping yard in Leatherhead," she reminiscences in her melodic Irish burr. "I got the job and we became firm friends. I soon discovered what an exceptionally talented horseman he was. It's unbelievable what he managed to achieve as an amateur. He was regularly beating some of the best jumpers around, all of whom were fulltime, fully-sponsored professionals. The other riders really respected him as an outstanding athlete. When he stopped competitive show jumping, it was because he had reached a pinnacle — he couldn't go any further against fulltime professionals. They did nothing else but ride horses, while he was competing in events and running a massive business at the same time. While other riders practised, he was holding down one of the most demanding jobs imaginable."

Dad also tried to get Deneys interested in riding. "It was one of James's few failures," recalls Deneys. "His horse's name was Trigger and it was an apt name as every time I got on his back it triggered a startling reaction which usually left me flat on my back — to James's unending enjoyment and laughter.

"James was an excellent horseman. I never got to grips with riding any horse and soon came to the realization that I could not drive anything that didn't have brakes. James convinced me that I would master the sport if we joined an English fox hunting group.

"Not to put too fine a point to it, this was another of his rare poor judgments. I disrupted the hunt so badly I was asked to leave. Thankfully horses and I parted company for good after that debacle. I was immensely relieved not to have suffered any serious injury."

Then, when my father was right at the top of his game, he got bored. A fundamental part of Dad's psyche was that he was always looking for new adventures and opportunities. I'm exactly the same. Once I have mastered one thing, I'm looking for another.

It can be a blessing, but also a curse.

In this instance it was a blessing for dad. He had done all he had set out to do. He was one of the most successful businessmen in England. He was a champion horseman. He had made his father proud.

It was now time to do something else. So he listed Federated on the London Stock Exchange, sold off his shares, and retired.

He then did what he had always wanted to do. He returned to Africa.

But not to the place he had dreamed about. It was not to the Valley of Heaven, as he had vowed to do as a schoolboy more than 20 years previously.

It was instead in Klaserie in the Limpopo Province.

Chapter 3

First home in Africa

PERHAPS ANOTHER REASON my dad decided to retire and up-sticks to Africa was that he and his first wife had recently split.

It was an amicable separation. My dad, his daughter and two stepsons from that marriage remained close to him. In fact, exceptionally close. Dad considered the boys his sons and I consider them my brothers despite the age gap.

Maybe the divorce, as well as being an alpha achiever for almost two decades in the often cut-throat property market, did fuel a type of burn-out. But even so, there is no doubt that most of all he wanted to return to the continent he loved,

He bought a large plot of land at the Klaserie Private Nature Reserve in what was then the Northern Transvaal, but today is the Limpopo Province, named after one of Africa's most iconic rivers.

Limpopo has some of the finest bush country on the planet and boasts a number of world class game reserves, the Kruger National Park being the most famous. Although Klaserie is private land, today it has unfenced borders with Kruger, ensuring a high density and healthy diversity of animals.

It's also one of the largest private reserves in the country, spanning more than 60,000 hectares. Apart from being home to the Big Five — elephant, rhino, buffalo, lion and leopard — it also boasts impressive herds of giraffe, zebra, warthog, hyena, baboon, hippo, impala, kudu, waterbuck, wildebeest and cheetah.

If you are lucky, you may even see packs of highly endangered wild dog, as well as the incredibly tough honey badger, the ultimate thug of the bush. Honey badgers look like small wolverines and they invented fighting dirty. They have been known to kill buffaloes — more than 10 times their size — by the simple expedient of going for the testicles.

In short, for an animal lover like Dad, this massive variety of wildlife in an unspoiled wilderness was paradise.

Once he had bought his plot, he started building a camp where he would live out in the wild for much of the year. I can imagine him being as happy as a lion basking in the African sun. He was back in the bush and now had the money to enjoy it.

I think at this stage of his life he needed to regroup and reassess where he was going. He had soared to dizzy heights as a businessman, been a champion show jumper, and had always lived life at full steam. He had not only achieved everything he had set out to do, he had excelled at doing it. He now wanted to relax for a bit.

But as I said before, things always happened when my father was around, whether spontaneously or otherwise. Chilling out was not his natural condition. He may have wanted to slow down, but that's not what transpired.

Dad became firm friends with the head ranger of Klaserie, a bush legend called Erwin Liebnitz. At the time, the area was crippled by one of the worst droughts in living memory. Wild animals were dying of thirst in their scores. Skeletons and sun-bleached bones lay scattered across vast tracts of desiccated wilderness. It was up to a handful of committed men of the wild such as Erwin to prevent what was turning into a mass kill-off.

The best way to save animals when water holes dry up is the obvious one; relocate them to wetter areas. This was backbreaking work as the animals had to be corralled into a boma — a livestock stockade — and then herded onto trucks through specially constructed funnels. They would then be driven to where rains were more plentiful.

The most effective method of corralling wild animals was by helicopter, and a new breed of aviator, similar to crop sprayers and daredevil barnstormers, was born. These chopper pilots would fly just metres off the ground, risking hitting trees and power lines, while coaxing herds of highly agitated animals into capture pens against their will. A skilful chopper pilot could shepherd skittish animals in the bush like a highly-trained sheepdog.

But you needed nerves of steel, a rock-steady hand, and — dare one admit it? — a love of danger. In other words, someone like my father.

A capture outfit called Fauncap was already established at Klaserie when Dad arrived, run by a game ranger, Thys

Maritz and a veterinary surgeon called Blackie Swart. Also with them was a tough, fun-loving, young ranger called Les Carlisle.

Blackie could fly helicopters, but it wasn't ideal to have the vet up in the air when corralling frightened animals on the ground. Also, Blackie had to monitor animals that had been tranquilised. So when Thys and Blackie discovered that Dad had a helicopter licence, they were ecstatic. It took a few minutes watching him in action to see that he was an exceptional flyer. Even better, as far as they were concerned, he offered to buy their helicopter and fly it on capture missions. Again, they couldn't believe their luck.

Then when Dad looked at their business plan, which by their own admission was drawn up by hard men of the bush rather than suave men in suits, Dad sorted that out for them as well.

It was a match made in heaven. The capture team got an ace pilot and businessman, while Dad got a daily dose of adrenalin doing two things he loved; flying choppers and working with animals.

He also cabled his horse yard manager in Surrey, Carolyn Boyd, telling her to close the stables for the summer and come and work at Klaserie.

"I asked what he wanted me to do as it was obvious he was not going to be show jumping in the African bush," recalls Carolyn. "He laughed and said what he actually needed was someone to cook for the guests in the bush. It sounded wildly exciting, so I packed my bags.

"It was a fantastic experience, one of the highlights of my life. These men were doing hard, dangerous work and there was always an electric buzz of energy in the camp. James loved every second of it. This was the flying he was born to do."

The dangers of wild animal capture were many and any mistake could be fatal. Not surprisingly, Dad was involved in two serious crashes. Les Carlisle, the youthful ranger who was living the dream in the wild witnessed them both.

"The first happened when James was flying low, which in game capture is most of the time," said Les. "His tail rotor nicked the branch of a tree and we watched in horror as the chopper lurched and then started spinning like a top. Somehow, against all odds, James managed to get the machine down the right way up. We expected the worst, but to our astonishment, a few minutes later he calmly walked out of the wreckage. His only injury apart from being battered and bruised was a nasty gash on the head. It was one of the most stunning displays of flying I have seen, even though the machine was a total write-off.

"We rushed him to camp where we had a biltong factory and put him on the stainless steel table used for butchering animals. One of the guys said, 'Hey James, you know what happens to animals that go on these tables? I'd be worried if I was you!'

"James was laughing all the time. He wasn't getting much sympathy — but that gallows humour is what he loved."

The vet and co-owner of the company, Blackie Swart used his expertise on animal injuries to stitch the wound.

Les continued, "Blackie examined the gash on James head, which was still bleeding heavily, and said, 'I've got good news and bad news'."

"What do you mean?" asked James.

"Well," said the Blackie, "The good news is I can see right into your head."

"So what's the bad news?"

"There's nothing inside."

"James guffawed like a drain. He loved this banter."

There was a party at the camp that night, and after his rudimentary surgery on a butcher's table, Dad and the rest of the capture crew went off to celebrate that he was still alive. Despite being a little groggy and still shaking off the effects of a local anaesthetic, probably one that was usually used on wild animals, legend is that Dad was the last man standing among the revellers.

"James wasn't going to let something as trivial as a chopper prang spoil his fun," Les said.

Two weeks later his stitches were removed on the same butcher's table. The entire treatment for an injury from a potentially fatal crash was performed in an abattoir.

The second accident was equally harrowing. Game capture aviation in those early days was ground-breaking seat-of-the pants stuff involving aerodynamics, spins and turns that few pilots would ever be called upon to do. Which meant that there were no guides or 'how to' books.

On this occasion, there was so much heat and dust in the air that Dad could not gain altitude once he had taken off. He had no alternative but to crash-land.

That in itself was a major problem. But even worse was that he crashed in the middle of a herd of buffalo, who were somewhat bemused — and not surprisingly upset — by a human falling from the sky and disturbing their midday rest.

There was not much the people on the ground could do. They couldn't just 'shoo' off a herd of agitated buffalo, one of the most dangerous creatures in the African bush.

Undeterred, Dad calmly shut down the engine and waited for the buffalo to give him enough space to make a dash for safety.

The helicopter was a complete write off. As in the previous crash, Les Carlisle said it was only Dad's superb flying skills that got him out largely unscathed.

However, being a helicopter pilot in the bush had other advantages, not just chasing animals. The chopper was equally useful for less perilous chores. Both Dad and Les were keen hockey players, but the team they played for was at the Air Force Base at Hoedspruit 30 miles away. No problem

— they arrived at club matches like celebrities in Dad's chopper.

"It was great fun," recalls Les. "Everyone thought James was an absolute legend. I'm not sure if players have ever rocked up for a game in a chopper since then."

Every now and again Dad would return to civilisation, and on one occasion he visited Cape Town, arguably South Africa's most beautiful city. A friend there had an attractive blonde daughter. Her name was Mandy Nichols and, like my dad, she was passionate about horses.

Mandy was 18 at the time, 22 years younger than Dad. "I had never met James, even though my family knew him well," she recalled. "So my mother insisted that I come along and say hello. I wasn't enthusiastic as I had just started a job with a medical technology firm and had to take a day off just to meet some guy from England."

That lack of enthusiasm disappeared the moment Dad walked into the room

"I took one look at him and something in my head said 'you're going to marry this man'. He was handsome, friendly and charming, and I knew we were destined to be together."

Dad later told me of that first meeting. He said Mandy's 'wonderfully natural' beauty and cute timidity was as refreshing as a sparkling mountain stream. She was stunning looking, but completely unaware of it. For a sophisticated man of the world with film star looks, Dad was bowled over in an instant.

Mandy had been brought up on a stud farm just outside Cape Town which specialised in breeding thoroughbred Arabian horses, and it was soon obvious that the attraction between them was mutual, sparked by their strong equestrian bond. Dad encouraged Mandy to hone her skills further and suggested she went to the Equitation School in England where he had contacts.

"I took his advice and we regularly kept in touch," Mandy said. "In fact, I even looked after his ex-wife's stud farm in Surrey while she went on holiday."

Dad was also in England at the time.

"It was there that we got to know each other and he asked me to come and work at his game camp.

"I went back to Cape Town and told my mother I was going to Klaserie for six months. She was not happy as she thought I was neglecting my fledging career as a medical technician. But I was adamant. I was not going to miss this wonderful opportunity. For me as a young woman, working on a game ranch would be a university of life experience. I may not get another chance to do it."

It was hard, healthy, physical outdoor work, clearing bush and cutting down mopane trees in often stifling sub-tropical heat to make an airfield. Mandy loved every minute of it.

The inevitable happened. Despite the age difference, Dad and Mandy fell in love and got married. It happened just as Mandy had instinctively known from the moment she met this suave Englishman who, ironically, was most at home in the African bush. Soon afterwards, she became my mum.

However, tragedy struck the day they arrived home from honeymoon.

They were driving around a bend in the bush and Mum remarked that there seemed to be a lot of smoke in the distance.

Dad agreed. "Must be a veld fire," he said.

Then as they got closer, Mum remarked it seemed to be frighteningly close to their camp.

In fact, it was their camp. The rondavels and other buildings were all on fire.

The fire had started when a staff member lit the 'donkey' — a traditional rural water-heating system — with paraffin instead of wood. The highly-inflammable liquid exploded with a 'whoosh' and within seconds the fire spread.

"Then nearby gas cylinders exploded and the fire was raging out of control," said Mum. "We did our best to douse it, spraying the blaze with hoses and tossing bucket after bucket of water onto flames that were flaring everywhere. But it was like trying to plug a volcano. The inferno was gutting everything in its path.

"Then my room went up in flames. I still had my own quarters as we had only just got married. Within minutes, it was just cinders and ash."

Mum and Dad watched in shock as almost everything they owned was razed to the ground.

It was an ominous start to married life. But my parents responded in typical fashion, rebuilding the entire gutted camp, brick by brick. The newly-married couple started their life together by having to restore their destroyed home from ashes.

This was made even more problematic as not long afterwards, my mother fell pregnant with me. Although I wasn't the eldest son in the broader sense, with Dad's two much-loved stepsons, I would soon be Dad's first blood son.

But it nearly didn't happen. Both my mother and I almost died when she gave birth.

"Living way out in the bush meant that I hardly even saw a gynecologist," Mum said. "But I sailed through pregnancy with no outward problems and so was given a clean bill of health. My doctor, who lived 500 miles away in Durban, said he would see me when I was due.

"Then everything went horribly wrong. I had developed placenta previa, which no one noticed.

"At first I just thought my waters had broken. But when I started bleeding badly, we realised something was seriously wrong. I was bleeding to death.

"It was then a mad rush to the intensive care unit where I had an emergency blood transfusion, followed by an equally urgent caesarian.

"The doctors only just managed to get Peter out in time as he had already stopped breathing. He was put on a ventilator which managed to get oxygen into his lungs. It was a close call for both of us."

It didn't end there. Doctors discovered that due to the birth complications, I also had a hernia. This meant another emergency operation. I still have the scar on my belly button.

A year later Mum was pregnant with my younger brother, Jamie, and my parents started to reassess their lives out in the wild at Klaserie.

It was then that Dad decided to revisit the Eden of his youth; Karkloof, the valley of heaven.

Fortuitously – or was it destiny? – the property was for sale.

Dad could not believe it. He had vowed as a 16-year-old schoolboy standing on a hill overlooking paradise that one day he would own the Valley of Heaven.

Could that now actually happen?

Chapter 4

Karkloof

I LIVED A CHARMED LIFE as a toddler. Before I was a year old, I had already faced death three times. Not that I played any heroic part in defying the Grim Reaper, of course. I was just 'there', so to speak.

The first was my complicated birth which nearly claimed the life of my mother as well.

I also don't remember the second, but I'm told it was equally nightmarish, if that is possible.

I was about eight months old at the time. My Mum was in the kitchen at Klaserie and she called out to Dad, "James, have you got PG?"

PG was my nickname, as those are my initials: Peter Grant.

"No, you've got PG," Dad shouted back.

My mother's blood ran cold. It was what every parent in a hot climate dreads. She instinctively knew what had happened and ran straight out to the swimming pool.

There I was, in the water.

But instead of being face-down at the bottom, which is what happens in 99 per cent of these awful child tragedies, I was floating.

It was the biggest stroke of good fortune in my life. We had been on holiday in America the month before and my mother insisted that I take swimming lessons. Even though I was a baby, she was adamant that I at least learn how to float. It may have been a subliminal instinct as her father had drowned, an awful family tragedy that happened when she was a teenager, but I don't know. All I do know is that her insistence saved my life.

Apparently, infant swimming lessons can be quite scary, both for the toddlers and their parents. It's genuine sink or swim stuff. The instructors dunk the babies in the water and bring them up floating on their backs. It's a literal baptism of fire, and my grandmother was pretty vociferous in her criticism of my parents. I think she couldn't bear the thought of her beloved baby grandson being 'traumatised'.

But no one questioned my mother's instincts after that. For instead of panicking and gulping in water after falling into the pool, I was doing the exact arm movements to keep myself afloat as I had been taught in America. There is no doubt I would have drowned otherwise.

The nightmare for my parents wasn't yet over. A few months after they had recovered from the near-drowning shock, my mum went into the bedroom one afternoon to pick me up after my nap. There at the bottom of the crib was a coiled Egyptian cobra.

The highly-venomous snake was asleep, and so was I. At first Mum just stood rigid, frozen in fright. There was little else she could do. If she disturbed the reptile — or even worse, if I had woken screaming — it would almost certainly have reared up and sunk its fangs into me. The chances of an infant far out in the bush surviving a bite from an Egyptian — or snouted — cobra are zero.

Fortunately, the snake woke before I did, slithering off the crib and out of the room into the bush.

Perhaps it is stretching it slightly to say that was a near-death experience, but it certainly did help my parents make up their minds to move on from Klaserie.

For both of them, their lives there had run their course. My dad had done what he had set out to do by building a beautiful camp in the wilderness. The drought was now over and the game capture missions with all the adrenalin and exhilaration that this entailed had come to an end. Also, Dad had written off both his helicopters after two very close calls, so maybe he thought he was pushing his luck a little.

Mum, on the other hand, had had enough of extreme wilderness living, looking after one small child in a bush camp and with another on its way.

As soon as Dad saw Karkloof was on the market, he put in an offer. It was accepted. The Valley of Heaven was now his. That teenage vow made all those years ago had been fulfilled. All that hard work, all those long, gruelling hours running high profile companies, all that sweat and stress had been worth it.

Once the title deeds were signed, Dad hired a highly-skilled and inventive engineer called Dave Mitchell to construct his dream game reserve. The project of his life had now begun.

It's also where my life, as I remember it, started.

Dave, now retired and living with his wife in Plettenberg Bay in the Eastern Cape was just the man for the job. He recalls those early days well.

"James drove me to the reserve to show me around, and I have to admit that at first I was pretty unimpressed," he said. "The entrance was a flimsy farm gate with a rusty and barely legible 'No Entry' sign tied on with wire.

"This was no wilderness paradise. All I could see was a vast tract of overgrown bush with very little infrastructure, while the roads were just rutted tracks.

"The first thing we did was build a bridge across the Karkloof River, and then I understood James's vision. I understood what it was about the place that so fascinated James. We started to make that magic happen."

Karkloof today would be farmland if it wasn't for my father's vision. And it would have been an absolute travesty; a wildlife Shangri-La ploughed up into boring landscape to cultivate crops or pasture for cattle grazing.

The land is lush and fertile, naturally watered by the Karkloof River snaking through it. Although the area is called a mist-belt forest, in places it's almost tropical with grass plains and plenty of natural watering holes. It has everything needed for wildlife to flourish. It's a big, deep valley so no massive electric fences were needed to keep out poachers. The sheer scale of the steep cliffs is a daunting natural barrier. No one can get in or out without coming through the gates, so it's an idyllic God-made sanctuary for the animals to thrive.

It was my first home. I truly was born in the Garden of Eden. I don't think many children could have been brought up in such idyllic settings. There were no apple trees, but there were plenty of snakes. But even those could not detract from the Valley of Heaven.

The first stage of the project was to carve out roads to get at least a basic infrastructure. There is only one way to do this — hacking through dense bush, a time-consuming and, sadly, dangerous job. We lost a worker when a digger slipped over the edge of a road being hewn up a hill and crushed the driver to death.

Once the roads were finished, built with sweat and blood, Dad and Dave Mitchell designed chalets along the river banks, blending in naturally with the environment to be a hidden haven. It was the perfect getaway for people to forget the hassles and stresses of urban life and just relish being in the wild.

It was no coincidence that much of what Dad and Dave created was reminiscent of scenes from Out of Africa, as that was one of my dad's favourite films. That is what Dad envisaged. The game viewing camp on the river was so similar to the movie that you could almost picture Meryl Streep and Robert Redford picnicking there, sipping champagne. He called it Eagle Camp.

But to achieve this was no easy task. Karkloof was a lot of work for both my parents. It was a complex family business, whereas Klaserie had been a single camp, run more for enjoyment than as a money-making operation.

Mum was in charge of the chalets on the river. So in effect, she was not only looking after two young boys, but also the guests. My dad did what he loved best; managing wildlife.

There was little game on the reserve when we arrived so Dad started bringing in animals, not just locally but from around the world. He bought rare roan antelope breeding stock from the Czech Republic and also adopted three orphaned rhino calves.

But his biggest pride was a herd of disease-free Cape buffalo, some of which he brought home to Africa from Texas; others from the Whipsnade Zoo in London.

As anyone who understands wildlife will know, to have a disease-free buffalo herd in Africa is like owning gold. In those days it was unheard of.

The Cape buffalo is one of the hardiest animals on the planet and magnificently adapted to the harsh conditions of the continent. In fact, it has adapted so well that that it can be both a carrier of fatal sicknesses, such as foot-and-mouth, tuberculosis and tick-borne corridor disease, and immune at the same time. This means that these killer infections don't affect buffalo, but will kill off domestic cattle in their hundreds of thousands if there is any contact. So buffalo herds are restricted to remote parks and have to be kept well clear of any agricultural land.

Unless, of course, they are disease free.

Once Dad had his re-stocking programme in place, he phoned his old friend and hockey teammate from Klaserie, Les Carlisle. My dad saw huge potential in the energetic young ranger and wanted him on his team.

For Les, Karkloof presented a big opportunity to further his wildlife vocation. The bush was not just a job; it was his life.

"At that stage I had left Klaserie and was running my own game capture business," said Les. "Then I got this call from Jimmy saying he needed a wildlife manager, and I was the guy for the job

"The timing was perfect. Not only was it a big break career-wise for me, but I was also planning on getting married. However, my fiancée Lynette said she would not marry me while I was out catching wild animals all the time. So this was the ideal chance for me to settle down and move out of game capture into game management."

Another reason was that Les said he also regarded James as a 'conservation hero'.

"I first met him as a 19-year-old game capturer, and to me this big, suave, blonde helicopter pilot was really quite something. The fact that he had now bought a game reserve

— he didn't have to as he had independent financial means — really impressed me. He was such a passionate conservationist even though he was a millionaire. I had never met someone like that with such commitment to wildlife. So he really was one of my heroes."

Les accepted the job and also popped the question to Lynette.

"Thankfully, she said yes. We got married and straight after the wedding I moved to Karkloof. James told me to build a house wherever I wanted. It was a great start to our married life."

Les and James were soon breaking new ground in buying animals, many endangered, from other parts of the world. It was also immensely satisfying work re-introducing gene pools back to Africa.

"In many aspects, Karkloof was at the forefront of bringing in healthy new bloodlines," said Les. "When I fetched some disease-free buffalo from Texas and brought them to the Sun City game auction, they were the first privately-owned clean buffaloes in the country. The only other disease-free herd was in Addo Elephant Park near Port

Elizabeth that belonged to the South African National Parks."

But, said Les, SANParks wanted to keep their buffalo separate and were not interested in live game trading. Consequently, a little-known ranch deep in the KwaZulu-Natal Midlands was one of the few — if not only — reserves that could guarantee its animals were clean.

When the buffalo from Whipsnade Zoo first arrived at Karkloof, a local newspaper reporter claimed that they were 'not really buffalo'. Instead, he wrote that they were American bison. What the city journalist didn't know was that Cape buffalo will grow thicker coats in cold weather, and these had just arrived from winter in London. I think they also got confused as Les had brought out Cape buffalo from Texas on an earlier occasion.

"We had a good laugh at that," said Mum. "They soon shed their coats in the African sun."

Dad was also keen on breeding other endangered species such as roan and sable.

"We bought breeding stock in from the zoo in Prague," said Les. "What I learnt from bringing in buffalo gave us a running start in setting up other projects. In those days,

Karkloof was, with other notable reserves, at the forefront of re-introducing species."

At that stage the Karkloof Falls Game Reserve was purely an animal viewing reserve with overnight accommodation and a picnic area. People came both locally and from around the world for a spiritual wilderness experience in the Valley of Heaven. Like the animals, the reserve flourished.

It was almost too good to be true.

Unfortunately, it was. Ironically, this time it was too much rain, not lack of it. Just as Dad had arrived at Klaserie in the middle of one of the country's most crippling droughts, in 1987 some of the worst floods in living memory thundered down the Upper Umgeni and Karkloof Rivers, demolishing everything in their path with the wrath of a tsunami.

It was a sight to behold; forces of nature, unimaginably savage, being unleashed with cataclysmic ferocity. Boulders the size of double-story buildings were hurled down torrential waterfalls like pebbles. Giant, ancient hardwood trees, uprooted as easily as you would pick a tuft of grass, splintered like matchsticks as they were tossed down steep gorges raging with angry swirling floodwaters. Hills that had stood as sentinels overlooking the valley for millennia imploded as avalanches of mud surged down the cliffs as lethal as lava from a volcano.

Eagle Camp looked as though it had been nuked. There was nothing left. Not one structure was still standing. The chalets, lovingly crafted to blend in with the bush, were smashed beyond recognition.

Dad was in America at the time and Dave Mitchell phoned with the awful news. He took it in his stride, merely asking Dave if they were insured.

They weren't. As the floods were deemed an act of God, the insurance company would not pay out.

He returned home on the next available flight. He and Mum drove home and stood on the kopje overlooking the valley and surveyed the scene of utter destruction below, stunned to their souls. In one awful day, their business had been wiped out. Everything they had worked for had been destroyed.

Once more, just as they had done after the inferno at Klaserie, they had to start again from scratch. They had to rebuild not only the camp, but their lives.

This time Dad wanted to do something different with the reserve. He wanted to make wildlife accessible to all. He wanted everyone who came to Karkloof to have a special experience and encounter the amazing animals that lived there.

Dad had visited many game parks in the country and knew from firsthand experience that just because you paid your money, it didn't mean you would see animals.

Unless the rhinos, wildebeest, buffaloes and zebra obliged by being close to the road, you could drive for hours and just see bush.

He wanted to change that. He wanted a quality wilderness experience to be for everyone, not just the purists or the rich. He believed that the future of wildlife was directly proportional to the number people who benefited from that experience.

So he came up with a new idea. Something so radical that it had never been tried on a game reserve before. He envisaged a Disney-style theme park in the bush that all could enjoy.

It would be a wilderness experience for the masses excluded from the hugely expensive private game reserves.

He would call it Safari World.

It would be the second phase of life at Karkloof for my family.

Mum and Dad

Mum, me and Jamie and (below) with Dad

Baby me watching a warthog with a monkey 'jockey' being fed

(below) Jamie and I climbing trees

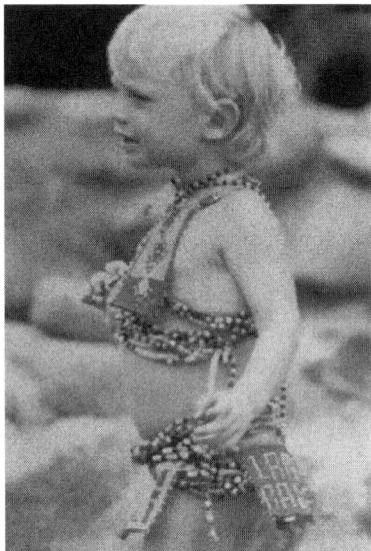

With good friend Brent Leo-Smith and (above) in my Zulu
outfit.

Chapter 5

Snakes

SNAKES ARE SYNONOMOUS with Africa. But I suppose that is to be expected. You cannot have Gardens of Eden without snakes.

From the black mamba, one of the most venomous to the puff adder, one of the most belligerent, there's a golden rule: don't mess with them.

To make it worse for me, I have a phobia of snakes. As I have mentioned, my first introduction to these slithery creatures was in my crib, so perhaps it's subliminal. Or perhaps it's voodoo — I actually am jinxed. They seem to like coming for me.

The cobra in the cot was not the only serpent scare we had in Klaserie when I was a toddler. We had them often. On one occasion my dad had been working in the aircraft hangar and as he walked out into the garden he stepped over what he thought to be a hosepipe.

He did this several times, walking in and out of the hangar. Then as he was about to step over it again, the hosepipe moved. It was the biggest, thickest, meanest black mamba either he or my Mum had ever seen. Mambas are fiercely territorial, so it was ever more terrifying for my parents to discover one so big that it could be mistaken for a hosepipe near the house with their baby son inside.

Mambas are among the most lethal snakes in the world, but Dad had another encounter with an equally sinister killer at Klaserie while relaxing under a tree. He was almost dozing off when a twig snake glided off a branch onto his shoulder and then down his arm.

A twig snake — also called a vine snake — is dangerous because no anti-venom has been discovered. Although bites are rare, they cannot be treated and thus are almost always fatal. So even if it doesn't kill you as quickly as a mamba, it's just as deadly.

It was a strange sensation, Dad said, as the snake was so expertly camouflaged that at first he thought it was a stick. He only knew he had a problem when it moved.

There was a low branch next to him, and with remarkable presence of mind he decided the best plan would be to coax the snake to crawl onto that. Moving his arm as slowly as possible, barely an inch every few seconds, he extended his hand until it reached the branch. The snake seemed in no hurry to move off, but eventually slithered along his arm onto the branch and back up the tree.

Dad later said it was scary in the extreme, yet at the same time, a strangely beautiful moment. I don't know whether I would have been that philosophical with a venomous reptile camouflaged as a twig sliding down my arm.

Another scare was when Mum was in England and talking to Dad on a radio-phone. He suddenly whispered, "I'll call you back."

Mum was immediately suspicious — did Dad have another woman in his room? She insisted that they continue talking. Dad cut her off.

About 10 minutes later he phoned back to say that a spitting cobra had suddenly reared up at him. It was right by the phone. He'd had to move out of its way — fast.

So Mum decided that with one young baby which had nearly died twice, another on the way, snakes the length of hosepipes and spitting cobras interrupting telephone conversations, she'd had enough of Klaserie.

However, unknown to her Karkloof would be just as wild. It may have been closer to big towns, but when Dad bought the reserve it was completely overgrown, even though the valley was just as gorgeous as when he had first seen it all those years ago.

In fact, Mum tells the story of meeting the previous owner just before the purchase went though. With many of the creepy-crawly incidents at Klaserie still vivid in her mind, she asked him if there were snakes in the valley.

To her horror, he nodded. There were plenty. In fact, he said he had seen three green mambas in the tree by the kitchen a couple of weeks ago.

This was not what Mum wanted to hear. In fact, as far as she was concerned, he could not have painted a grimmer picture of our new home if he'd tried. No doubt he was keen to sell his property, but he had just given what must be one of the worst sales pitches in the world.

Mum turned to my dad and said there was no way she was going to live at Karkloof. But Dad, who could charm an Eskimo into an ice investment, eased her fears.

Anyway, we knew that green mambas are only found in coastal areas, not in the Karkloof mist forests, so this was wrong information. The snakes were almost certainly boomslangs, which are also highly venomous, but timid and seldom attack humans.

However, it's unrealistic to live in the bush and not expect to encounter snakes. Mum, who's pretty tough and at home in the wild, certainly knew that. But fear of snakes is far more rampant than snakes themselves. Even in the more remote parts of Africa, you are still statistically more likely to die of sickness, or even a bus crash, than from a snake bite.

Well…that's what I keep telling myself. Except in my case, I have a damn good reason for my almost morbid fear of snakes. In fact, two good reasons. I have been bitten twice. I still have nightmares about it.

My first conscious run in with a snake was when I was with my best friend Pugga. We were about five years old and had packed some food in our knapsacks, grabbed our assegais, bows and arrows like true Zulu warriors and cruised off into the bush.

We came across a large boulder; requiring a steep 10-foot climb to the top. We sat there for a while, then jumped down the other side. Almost waiting for us at the base of the big rock was the mother of all puff adders. We first heard it's distinctive 'puff', a malevolent sibilant explosion that even today gives me goosebumps. Then we saw it, a yard of tan-brown muscle as thick as our arms with white and black chevrons running down its back. It was a fat boy all right, coiled into a S-shape and warning us not to approach.

It was a warning we heeded. For the moment, anyway.

The next day Pugga and I returned to the boulder and started searching for the snake again. We were inquisitive and wanted to get a closer view. The brush with a puffing brute had given both of us a massive rush — I still remember it vividly, even though I was only five years old. That tingling blast of adrenaline is like nothing else.

It wasn't as if we were ignorant of the potential consequences. We knew that if we were bitten it would be life-threatening as, apart from a puff adder's highly-toxic necrotic venom, we were about three miles from home. But the buzz of coming face-to-face with such a savage creature was part of the excitement of growing up.

Puff adders were pretty much part of bush life. Mum had a close call on her morning jog in the valley one day when she almost stepped on one. At the last minute she managed to use her momentum to jump over it, just as it struck. Fortunately, it missed, but she certainly did a record time sprinting around the valley that morning.

More people die from puff adder bites than from any other snake in Africa, but this is mainly because it is the most widespread species. In her famous book 'I Dreamed of Africa', Italian-Kenyan author Kuki Gallman describes the heart-breaking death of her only son Emanuele from a puff adder bite while milking the snake for anti-venom. He was only 17 at the time and had been studying to become a herpetologist.

Obviously neither Pugga nor I told our mothers about our 'fat boy' puff adder escapade, as we would have been banned from exploring in the bush on our own.

Two years later I got my first bite, possibly by another puff adder, but we'll never really know. It was at the reserve's visitors' centre on the river, where one of the highlights was speeding down a run-off from a dam into a whirlpool, then back into the river. The ride lasted about three or four minutes and on one occasion I came off the tube in the whirlpool. I started swimming after it with the current ripping me downriver when, to my horror, I saw a snake on the river bank just ahead. I was in the grip of the river and had no control of where I was going. The snake slid into the water exactly where I was headed. It was surreal; I could see exactly what was going to happen — that the snake and I would collide — but I couldn't do anything about it.

We crashed into each other. It wrapped itself around my foot as fast as a whip. I felt a quick stab on my toe like a needle jab. My heart went cold.

Then it was gone.

I went into shock. All around me, people were running away shouting, 'snake, snake!' I just froze on the river bank, unable to move.

I knew I was in big trouble. I was far from the main building where my mum was at the restaurant and started panicking, believing that I would die before help arrived. Or at the very least lose my foot. Even though I was only seven-years-old, even though I was in shock, I understood the starkness of the situation with cold clarity.

Then a man, a stranger who had been visiting the reserve with his family, rushed over. He asked where my mother was. I said my parents owned the place. My voice sounded weird, echoing far away in my head as if someone else was speaking.

He picked me up, put me on his shoulders and sprinted to the restaurant which was about a mile away. All I remember was that he was tall and was the only person who came to help when everyone else was running in other directions. He was an absolute hero. None of us even knew his name. We never saw him again.

My mum put out an emergency radio call and our wildlife manager Les Carlisle arrived soon afterwards. The biggest problem was Les could not give me anti-venom serum until he knew what snake had sunk its fangs into me.

And that was the scariest part — it happened so fast that I had no idea what type of snake it was. All I remembered was that it was short, dark and fat and its head was triangular-shaped, almost like a diamond. Ominously, for most Africa hands, that description means one thing; puff adder. The word 'dark' was confusing as 'puffs' are usually a dusty brown colour with darker chevrons. But the consensus was that maybe it looked darker because it was in the water.

This was now deadly serious. Everything pointed to the reptile being a puff adder, but Les couldn't risk given me antitoxin without being sure. Wrong serum can kill you quicker than an actual bite.

The word went out, "Find the snake that bit PG."

All staff dropped what they were doing and rushed to the river, but the snake had long gone. It had either swum downstream or was deep in the bush on the far bank.

Everything ground to a standstill. It was as though there had been a shark attack on a beach and everyone was freaking out not knowing what to do — including my poor mother.

Fortunately, Les took charge. He lay me down outside the restaurant and dried me off. Then I started to sweat. Mum tried to keep me cool, but perspiration steamed off as if I was in a sauna.

Soon I started getting headaches, which combined with heavy sweating caused huge concern. There was no time to take me to hospital. The trip could have caused more stress, which was exactly what Les was trying to avoid. Without knowing what snake had bitten me, there was little any doctor could do that was not already being done by Les. It was just a waiting game to see what would happen next and treat symptoms as they appeared. When you don't know the species of the snake, you have to be reactive rather than proactive.

After a while the wound turned red, looking more like a wasp sting. But the good news was there was no sign of tissue rot that would have come from a puff adder bite.

Les was superb at calming my mother's fears. For a start, he's a snake expert and as a schoolboy caught some of the deadliest species to sell for pocket money. In fact, Les had been bitten by a puff adder himself, so knew first-hand what to look out for.

"Panic is your worst enemy as shock can mask other vital symptoms," recalls Les. "So I told Mandy to put the kettle on, have some tea, and we'll just wait.

"After about half an hour, I started to relax. I was reasonably sure that Peter would be okay. There were no serious symptoms, apart from sweating. So I figured that if the snake had been a puff adder, it was a dry bite.

"Snakes often don't inject venom in a bite as they're not trying to eat you, they're trying to make you go away. They don't want to waste poison needed to kill food on something inedible like a human.

"But even if it wasn't a dry bite, we still had time on our hands. Puff adder poison, which breaks down muscle tissue, only starts showing serious damage after a couple of hours. I was waiting for Peter to start screaming about red hot pokers being stuck into his foot — because believe me, that's exactly what it feels like. If he wasn't feeling that pain, it wasn't a full-blown bite.

"On the other hand, if it had been a cobra bite, which attacks the nervous system, we would have seen symptoms right away."

Whatever snake it was, I soon recovered. If not a dry puff adder bite, some of the staff thought it may have been a mildly poisonous water viper, which were common down by the river.

But the nightmare was not over.

Three months' later I was walking along a bush path with my brother Jamie, when I noticed a patch of tall grass strangely 'quivering' about four or five yards ahead.

Everything else was still. There was no wind blowing, so why was just one small patch twitching?

I stopped and pointed it out to Jamie.

"What the hell is that?"

We just stared. It was the most bizarre thing we had seen. A line of grass moving on its own. At first I thought it was a field mouse or some other rodent. Then the 'quivering' started heading straight for me.

Suddenly a thin green snake darted into the path and launched itself at me, sinking its fangs into my ankle.

It was the same foot that had been bitten in the river. I fled in absolute horror. But I sprinted off so quickly that the snake didn't have time to withdraw its fangs and was still hooked to my foot.

My brother watched in awe as I sprinted towards our house with an attached snake flapping behind. He said I ran for about 40 yards, but to me it seemed more like 400, and I did so faster than Usain Bolt. It was only when I reached a small wooden bridge that the snake was snagged on a plank and yanked off.

As I felt it release, I looked behind. The snake just lay in the path for a moment, as much in shock as I was. Then it slithered back into the grass.

I can still picture it clearly to this day. It was more than four-foot long and light green, which everyone immediately imagines to be a green mamba. But I knew we don't get green mambas in Karkloof. I also knew it wasn't the equally dangerous boomslang as they live almost exclusively in trees and are back-fanged, which means it's difficult to bite a human on the foot.

It was instead a harmless grass snake. But harmless or not, it has given me more recurring nightmares than anything else. The scariest thing was that it wouldn't — or couldn't — let go of me. It was just hanging onto my foot like something from the worst horror movie you can imagine.

Jamie went running ahead and when I reached the house my mother was even more alarmed than she had been after the suspected puff adder bite. Even when I told her it was an innocuous grass snake, she didn't relax. You couldn't blame her. She had barely recovered from the shock of me being bitten just three months earlier.

We had a lot of other incidents with snakes, such as cobras creeping out of guests' cupboards or adders curled up on a pillow just as someone was about to go to bed. Not to mention a reptile-loving ranger called Ross, who was also a practical joker. He loved nothing more than tossing a leguaan into the back of a pick-up when staff were sitting inside and watch the resulting melee.

But his epic stunt was once handing my mum a pizza box, and when she opened it, a baby python wriggled out. Even though pythons are not poisonous, my mother, not surprisingly, did not see the joke. Ross never did that again.

But it seems snakes in Africa will always haunt me. It's like being cursed by some form of juju.

In 2016 I went back to Karkloof after a 17-year absence to film a video of my returning to the Valley of Heaven where I grew up.

On the first night I went to my bedroom ready to hit the sack after a long day of travelling. There curled up on the floor was a night adder. It was right next to my bed. Although night adders are not in the same league as mambas or puff adders, they can still give you a nasty and extremely painful bite.

My phobia instantly kicked it; I wanted to run off as fast as I could. But this was my bedroom. If I didn't get rid of the reptile, where would I sleep?

Fighting my growing dread, I grabbed a nearby umbrella. It may have been bad luck opening it inside, but in my opinion having a snake in your room was infinitely worse luck.

Using the open brolly as a broom, I swept the reptile out of the building into the bush.

My dad had tried to cure my phobia. I was a child and had woken up one night to find our cat playing with a snake — also a night adder — on the floor about two feet away. If I had jumped out of bed, I would have landed on it.

The snake kept striking, but the cat was too fast. I screamed and Dad rushed into the bedroom.

He calmly got a broom and eased the wriggling reptile into a plastic bag. He then released it into the bush.

He came back to my room, put his arms around me and dried my tears.

I asked why he hadn't killed the snake. He just said it wasn't hurting anyone, so why hurt it? That was the key lesson I learned that day. Dad always wanted to preserve creatures, no matter how dangerous. To him, a venomous snake was just as important in the wild as a cute-looking Nyala doe. At the moment I understood exactly what he meant and my respect for him rocketed. I also do not wish snakes any harm.

But having said that, nothing, but nothing, will cure my horror of snakes.

It's a phobia I have earned the hard way. This is not once bitten twice shy.

It's TWICE bitten.

Chapter 6

Africa's first Jurassic Park

A FTER THE FLOODS washed away my parents' dreams that had been built with cement and sweat, the second phase of Karkloof Reserve began.

It was called Safari World and it was to be an entirely new concept in wilderness vision and planning. My dad was experimenting with the best ways to bring wildlife to the person in the street, not an exclusive few. Safari World was out of the box thinking on a grandiose scale.

But the amount of work that first needed to be done in reconstructing the wreck of Karkloof after the Biblical-scale floods was staggering. We had to rebuild entire hills with tons of topsoil trucked in by fleets of lorries, as well as clearing rocks the size of houses and bulldozing through tangled rafts of splintered trees clogging the river like a congested motorway.

Dad called in his old friend Dave Mitchell, who had helped him build the initial bridges and camp, and outlined his vision for a new-style wilderness experience. The first thing they did was design a home for us at the top of the plateau with a panoramic view of the valley. Then they created Africa's first wildlife theme park.

It had funfair-type rides, shows, restaurants and playgrounds. Also, using giant boulders that had been flung like marbles down the raging river, Dad and Dave designed a natural dam with a fast flowing run-off where guests could go for exhilarating tube rides into an artificial whirlpool. This later became 'famous' as the place where I was first bitten by a snake.

There was nothing else anywhere in the bush like it. The best description would be to call it an African Jurassic Park. It had all the theme park stuff, but with real animals. There were warthogs wandering around while people picnicked, leguaans basking not far from where people were swimming or buying ice cream, tame elephants posing for photos, and a huge variety of wildlife, including lions which were kept separately in a vast enclosure. You could also go on a game drive around the reserve and see impressive herds of buffalo, giraffe, zebra and wildebeest. There were several rhinos as well, one called Big Boy because that's exactly what he was with a horn to match.

In other words, it combined a day of family entertainment with a wilderness ethos.

But despite the noble intentions of a new all-inclusive and affordable conservation park, Safari World opened on a tragic note.

Firstly, one of the hippos escaped from an enclosure. We obviously couldn't let any guests onto the reserve with a hippo on the loose. Hippos kill more people in Africa than any other creature, apart from the miniscule but deadly malarial mosquito. But that is because rural Africans use hippo paths to access rivers and if someone gets between a mother and baby, there are almost always serious, if not fatal, consequences. Hippos are deadly.

The obvious place for a hippo to take refuge would be the river, and that was where we found it. But not in a remote section where we could try and coax it out. It was in the dam near the entertainment area. Soon there would be children playing and romping in that exact spot, so we had to get it out fast.

Regrettably, the most effective way to do that under the circumstances was to shoot it.

This was one of the rare occasions we shot a large animal on the reserve, and my dad took it hard. The only other animals shot on Karkloof were a crazed ostrich and warthogs, which bred so prolifically that they had to be culled. These always ended up as a Sunday roast.

The unfortunate hippo's carcass was dragged out of the river and we opened the gates. There were queues outside as Dad's unusual project had already caught the public's imagination.

However, it had been raining all week and the river was up. There's a causeway about a mile outside our entrance gates on the road leading to the reserve, which is usually just a sluggish stream. However, on that day the water was flowing over it.

It wasn't dangerously high, but to be on the safe side we placed two game guards there to monitor the situation. There were also clearly visible water markers in the stream gauging the depth and showing motorists that the road was easily negotiable. Any car, not just Land Rovers or SUVs, could get through, and initially there were no problems.

Then a Volkswagen Kombi arrived with a load of children. The driver told the game guards she wasn't happy with the water level and wanted to test it herself by wading across. The guards showed her the markers and said all other vehicles had easily got through. But she was adamant. She said she had children with her and wanted to make sure.

For some reason, she let the kids out of the Kombi. While everyone's back was turned, a six-year-old wandered into the water just above the causeway. The child slipped and was sucked under the low bridge, trapped, and drowned.

It was awful. No words can describe it. The distraught woman blamed herself. It wasn't her child and she had to tell the parents what had happened. It's impossible to imagine such a dreadful dilemma. She was inconsolable.

However, despite that harrowing first day, Safari World took off like no other reserve before it.

The weekends were crammed with people. On one occasion we had 4,000 people celebrating New Year's Eve. It was incredible how successful it was.

My brother and I were a little bemused by it all. For us it was a sort of reverse tourism — just as my family would drive to Durban's beaches for a break from the bush, people from Durban were driving the opposite way to Safari World.

Business was massive but it was tough work for everyone. Mum toiled tirelessly in the restaurant, while Les had the added responsibility of animal management and crowd control. Dad, the inspirational force, worked non-stop keeping all balls up in the air. To run a theme park and a game reserve in tandem required a superhuman juggling act. I'm not sure many other people could have done it.

Yet despite the popularity, despite the crowds, Dad never lost sight of the fact that Karkloof was first and foremost a wildlife reserve. His vision was to create an environment where animals could grow and thrive, and at the same time ensure tourists got their money's worth.

He fervently believed we had to get people out of the city, expose them to wildlife and hopefully some would become future conservationists.

Make no mistake, there was opposition. There were plenty of sceptics out there, particularly old-fashioned game rangers not receptive to what they considered to be 'new-fangled' ideas.

Dad understood where the sceptics were coming from. For most people, game reserves are about peace and tranquillity, being at home in the bush with their primal inner selves. Safari World's theme park, with crowds and noise, was at the other end of the spectrum.

But if you cater only for the purists, you are preaching to the converted. You will not get new disciples. And to keep our wild spaces safe, Dad believed we needed more converts than solely the true-believers at the time.

The idea of Safari World was to provide the best of both worlds. If you wanted something for the kids, there was the wilderness theme park. Then you could go for a game drive, like on other reserves, except we guaranteed that you saw a wide variety of wildlife. Our rangers made sure of that.

If you stayed at the reserve, you did so in a villa that blended into the bush, enjoyed fine cuisine and were wowed by the beauty of the valley and the animals flourishing in it.

It was a tough act to pull off, yet Dad did it.

A key attraction at the amusement area were elephants brought to us by a remarkable man called Doug Groves, an American who fell in love with Africa.

Doug first came to South Africa in 1987. He was in charge of escorting a trio of elephants returning to their native continent by ship. They first stopped off in the Western Cape to feature in a film called 'Circles in the Forest', which portrayed an almost supernatural relationship between a woodcutter in the Knysna Forest and an elephant called Old Foot. Doug's animals were the 'stunt elephants', so to speak, and played key roles.

After the movie — which was very successful — the elephants needed a home, and Dad agreed that they could come to Karkloof. Doug arrived with them, and so we had Cathy, Benny and Abu as our resident pachyderms. They were tame and extremely friendly. You could even ride them.

Dad, later bought two orphan calves, Jabu and Thembi, from the Kruger National Park, and Doug cared for them as well. When they arrived, they were tiny (for elephants, that is) and had to be bottle fed under a lamp.

The gentle giants loved being at Karkloof which was a paradise for them. It was beautiful to watch how they formed a close-knit family, the adults immediately accepting the two infants, and Doug had a mystical rapport with them.

Doug also put on shows at Safari World, demonstrating the enormous intelligence of elephants to tourists. For many visitors, the elephants were the highlight of their trip. There must be thousands of families, both in South Africa and abroad, who have photos of themselves posing with the amiable Karkloof goliaths long before 'selfies' were invented.

The elephants also starred in an internationally famous IBM advert, with the adults helping Thembi climb a sand dune to the background music of the Hollies classic, 'He ain't Heavy'. It was one of the most popular South African TV clips ever aired.

Dad then introduced lion to Safari World, which was another massive highlight for tourists. But that also didn't go strictly to plan.

It was set to be a gala event and as usual when there was some fun and action on offer, Deneys Hattingh, his best friend, was there. Deneys recalls the big cat 'launch' well.

"James had invited a selection of local dignitaries to celebrate the occasion. For some reason, they arrived adorned in suits and ties.

"Then the big moment came — the giant cats were to be released into their enclosure for the first time.

"Except they hadn't read the script. They took one look at the assembled gathering and charged!

"What happened next was truly amazing. The dignitaries forgot their status and fled in all directions, knocking each other over in their attempts to place as much distance between themselves and the roaring lions. The ladies also left in much undignified fashion, skirts in the air and showing a good turn of speed. They climbed into their cars and left. The park was opened without them."

The panic and pandemonium was despite the fact that there were two sturdy game fences between the guests and the lions. No one was in any danger. But as I say, when my dad is around, things always 'happen', one way or another. In fact, for the rest of his life, Dad couldn't stop laughing whenever he recounted that story and the dignitaries fleeing in disorderly disarray. It certainly got Safari World much fun publicity.

Despite being fenced, the lion enclosure was huge. It was nothing like a zoo and the animals roamed freely with plenty of bush, trees and open space. The only zoo-like concession

Dad made was to allow visitors to watch at feeding time, which also was very popular.

Safari World had by now well and truly taken off with the public. It had enormous appeal, as the huge crowds every weekend proved. But perhaps more importantly, slowly but surely, Dad and his highly-respected wildlife manager Les Carlisle also started to win sceptical conservationists over. The old-school rangers eventually realised this was not some cheap gimmick, but serious wildlife management.

"We always worked with the Natal Parks Board (now Ezemvelo KZN Wildlife) and told them in advance what we were thinking and why we were thinking it," said Les. "Everything was done with their approval. We didn't build a single enclosure, not one structure, without their consent. In fact, they even used us for some of their game capture projects as we were pretty successful in relocating surplus animals.

"I also was sent by the NPB to inspect various circuses that were popular in those days and give advice about ethical animal treatment. The Parks Board liked what we were doing at Safari World, but not what the circuses were doing."

Les said the success of Safari World stunned even the committed Karkloof staff.

"The massive volumes of traffic showed that James was right. His plan to expose people to wildlife was working way better than expected. The queues lining up at the gates on public holidays were staggering."

To run a reserve catering for that number of people, ensuring they were having a good time as well as creating potential wildlife ambassadors for the future, took extraordinary skill. It needed a man of Dad's energy and vision to pull it off.

One of the key factors was that Les and Dad were like brothers, despite the 20-odd year age difference. They worked exceptionally well as a team, both in Klaserie and Karkloof.

Then it all changed. In 1990 Les got a job offer; one that he simply could not refuse. It was to build a prestige reserve called Phinda in Zululand.

"I went to discuss it with James. He was quiet for a moment, then said there was no way that I could turn down such a once-in-a-lifetime opportunity. That was James to the core — always wanting the best for everyone else. He saw straight away that Phinda would be a massive career path for me and gave his blessing."

There were also other factors. Safari World had been a roller-coaster journey, literally and metaphorically, but by now Les had had enough of crowds.

"Thousands of people every weekend was not what I had signed up for," he said. "Safari World had become a victim of its own success. I would have preferred to have fewer people in my life, and James knew that."

However, James had one stipulation. He asked that Les stay on until all the lion and hippo had been relocated. Dad had decided that with Les going, it would not be safe to have dangerous animals on the reserve with so many people around.

Les agreed and they started the difficult relocation process right away. As always with my father and Les, there were some riotous times in moving dangerous animals around the countryside to new homes.

On one occasion, while transporting a large lion in a pick-up truck, Les needed to refuel and drove into a garage.

"It was about 2 a.m. so things were pretty quiet," said Les. "The lion was in the back of the truck, which had a canopy so it could not get out.

"I had sedated it with Zoletil, a standard tranquiliser which allows the animal to wake up gradually. You can let it sit up and start licking itself before you are in danger, so you have time to give it another injection if necessary.

"I got out of the truck and told the petrol attendant to fill it up while I went to the toilet. The bathroom had a little window and I could see the attendant leaning nonchalantly against the pick-up.

"Then his whole body suddenly went rigid. He gave a bloodcurdling yell and jumped right out of his shoes, bolting down the road barefoot. Petrol was spewing all over the forecourt.

"I rushed out, and there was the lion inside the canopy licking the window. That was what the attendant had just seen. He must have thought he was hallucinating.

"It took me about 20 minutes to coax him back to finish filling my truck. He put his shoes back on and I can imagine him trying to explain his 'day at the office' when he got home to his family."

However, Les had an equally hairy experience himself. He was in the back of a truck with another drugged lion when the big cat started stirring while they were still travelling.

Dad and a ranger were in the front, oblivious to the drama unfolding behind. But with the increasingly alert lion in front of him, Les could not get to the window of the cabin to bang on it.

The lion was now waking up fast. So as a last resort Les stood up and using all his weight 'bounced' on the rear suspension. Dad looked behind to see why the vehicle was rocking like a boat, and there was Les doing a pogo-dance trying to catch his attention.

Dad stopped and Les leapt out of the back, quickly preparing another syringe of Zoletil. The animal was again tranquilised and they carried on the journey.

Like the lions chasing the dignitaries story, Dad could also never finish repeating this one as he was always laughing so hard.

With Les gone and all lion and hippo safely relocated to other reserves, Dad decided to take a long, hard look at his options.

His experiment with Safari World had succeeded beyond his wildest dreams. In fact, beyond everyone's wildest dreams. Tourists were arriving in increasing numbers, but the question was what sort of impact was that having on the wildlife. Had, as Les said, the theme park been too successful for its own good?

It was a valid question, and one which was playing heavily on Dad's mind at the time. Also, he had got bored and needed a change. He had achieved what no-one said he would be able to do, but also wanted to preserve the beauty of the reserve and the peace of the animals.

He decided to go back to basics. He would rebuild Karkloof as a traditional animal-centric game reserve.

When Dad makes up his mind, he moves quickly. Now that he decided to close Safari World and create a new reserve, he wanted it done 'yesterday'.

He phoned Dave Mitchell, the engineer who had helped him with all his Karkloof projects, and Dave recalls the conversation going like this.

"Dave, I am fed-up with people coming onto the reserve, using the facilities free of charge and leaving their mess for us to clean up. I have decided to close Safari World down."

"I asked what he wanted me to do. 'You heard me,' he replied. 'When I come back in a few weeks' time I want to see the bush restored and no trace of the buildings whatsoever.'

"So having spent so much time in helping him to create Safari World, I then set about restoring the reserve to its original beauty."

That's what happened. The amusement park and restaurants were bulldozed down and Dad and Dave converted our house into a guest lodge with luxury *en suite* bedrooms, a conference centre and guest villas.

This was the third stage of Karkloof. It was once again a five-star game reserve, but Dad kept prices down as much as he could. His belief that conservation should be affordable was paramount. If anything, Safari World had strengthened his commitment to that.

We called it Game Valley. The name says it all.

Chapter 7

Game Valley

T HE THIRD STAGE OF Karkloof Nature Reserve under my dad was, I think, the one we all enjoyed the most.

No longer were we a theme park within a game reserve. We were now what Dad had originally intended Karkloof to be; an African wilderness. All vestiges of Safari World that did not fit in my dad's new vision were demolished. It was back to being the tranquil valley that he had first seen and fallen in love with as a schoolboy.

But even something as minimalistic as reverting to nature was done in my father's inimitable style. In other words, with open-arm exuberance. Every cent he had made from the

---

hugely successful Safari World venture was ploughed back into blending a truly African experience with five-star service. Apart from the refurbished luxury lodge, we now had a deluxe conference centre, 14 villas and an a-la-carte dining room.

My mum was in charge of catering, something she was exceptionally good at. She was a natural foodie, remarkable for a farm girl whose main passion had been horses. Even more remarkable is how slim and athletic she managed to keep herself despite all the fine cuisine.

She catered for huge conference groups, both internationally and from all over South Africa. A key attraction was the Game Valley Sunday Spit Roast and game drives, that became famous in the area. Guests would enjoy a massive spread of gourmet food, before being driven through the valley among rhino, buffalo, and impressive herds of nyala and impala. In the early days the elephants sometimes made an appearance during lunch, or could be heard nearby, their trumpet calls echoing through the valley.

With Game Valley, my dad injected his usual outside-the-box creativity and forged a new business model, even though we were reverting to our conservation roots. He had achieved all he had set out to do with Safari World and shown that a

Disney approach to conservation can work, as long as core ethics and standards of wildlife management are rigidly adhered to. But now that he had done that, he didn't want to be part of it anymore. At heart, my dad loved untamed places, in both a physical and mental sense. A theme park with loads of people, even in a reserve as vast as Karkloof, detracted from that. He wanted to revert to Africa in the raw again.

However, for most people that meant rustic camps perhaps a notch or two above tents and a blanket, rudimentary meals around the fireside, plastic chairs and tables and being at least a tad uncomfortable. The amalgamation of luxury and conservation was not always synonymous.

Dad thought otherwise. The old wilderness concept of being cold, wet and excited rather than warm, dry and bored, did not ring true. Why not be warm, dry and excited?

The core of his new business model was luxury and wildlife at affordable prices. People interested in a family get-away were his focus market. Although, those were not normally the most affluent customers, Dad wanted to be generous in sharing the Africa he loved.

To visit a private game reserve in Africa is a costly exercise; there's no getting away from it. The main reason is the inescapable fact that running a game reserve is ruinously expensive — from staff salaries to fencing off hundreds of square kilometres and incessant maintenance requiring heavy equipment needs a bottomless pit of cash.

But Dad had not been one of London's most innovative businessmen for nothing. As his best friend Deneys quipped, he had the Midas touch. He did deals with global tour operators and travel agents that kept our rooms fully booked for most of the time.

Dad also was a superb host, and parties at the reserve were legendary. People who came to see animals ended up having loads of fun along the way.

However, I don't think Dad knew how festive some of the festivities at Game Valley would get. If he did, he would not have designed the lodge so that his and Mum's room was directly above the bar.

As a property developer, Dad knew what good construction designs were all about. The lodge was beautifully positioned looking over the entire valley up to the Karkloof Waterfall. It was also the most photogenic spot in the entire area and even today there must be thousands of 'selfies' in photo-albums around the world taken from the spot.

Unfortunately, the lodge, for all its magnificence in blending in with the bush, was not one of the most practical buildings as far as my mum was concerned.

She had to wake at 6 a.m. every day of the week to be in the kitchen overseeing breakfast preparations. It was a long, hard day for her as she was continuously on her feet. By sunset, she was exhausted. She could think of nothing better than perhaps a nice cold sundowner and an early bed.

Fat chance of that. Down below in the bar, directly beneath the bed she had just collapsed on, the guests had different ideas. The noise and partying would often continue well into the next morning.

Mum would then have to get up bleary-eyed and supervise breakfast for more than 100 people after a sleepless night.

"We were on top of guests the whole time," she said. "Eventually I said to James I cannot live in this room anymore — I can't sleep."

My dad agreed. Only problem, where could they move to? The stylish *en-suite* bedroom he had lovingly designed could not be magically moved anywhere else. The villas were for guests, and usually fully booked, so it was not sound economic sense to commandeer one of those.

Eventually they moved into another room in the main lodge, close to where Jamie and I slept.

One evening a party in the bar got out of hand and some guests spilled over into our room. I use 'our room' lightly, as Jamie and I never really had our own room. We sort of 'hot-bedded' — we were moved around to different rooms according to the state of occupancy. Full occupancy meant we had to find somewhere else to sleep, which could be anywhere. I had my first proper 'own room' when I was about 19. Jamie probably even later as he ended up in the military.

My mum heard the commotion in her children's bedroom and sent Dad out to persuade the extremely jovial guests to leave as quietly as possible. As he had been fast asleep, he arrived rubbing his eyes and the only piece of kit he wore was a towel loosely knotted around his waist.

He politely requested the guests to return either to the bar or their villas. While doing so, his towel dropped. So there he was, stark naked, asking people a little worse for wear to move on.

This was not the most dignified bargaining position to be in. For some reason, they listened.

However, the story got out and there was much muffled hilarity when he walked into the dining room that evening. Particularly when one guest shouted, "Hey James, is that you?"

Dad looked at him quizzically. "Yes?"

"Sorry. I didn't recognise you with your clothes on."

The entire dining hall exploded with laughter. Dad loved that raucous banter, which is why he was so popular with guests. You can have as many business models as you want, but unless the guy driving it is having as much fun as his customers, it may not work.

My brother Jamie was named after my father. He was born 18 months after me, so he too was a boy from the wild. Unlike me, he was not born in Africa. Instead, he was born at a hospital just outside Lord's Cricket ground in England, which perhaps accounts for the fact that he was a superb cricketer, playing for the Surrey County junior team. His middle name is Deneys, after Dad's best friend.

But there was one crucial difference. Although 18 months is little more than a blink in a lifespan, for youngsters out in the bush it is equivalent of several years in terms of strength, endurance and practical knowledge. There may be little between us now age-wise, but on Karkloof the physical discrepancy between a five-year-old and an almost-seven-year-old was massive. I could climb cliffs and boulders that Jamie could not. I could swim against river currents that he could not, and go on game captures two years before he could. I thus, solely by virtue of being a mere 18-months his senior, had more connection to the land.

We both loved Karkloof, but I was born at the stage when it was still undeveloped and grew up totally in the wild. Jamie's earliest memories were of the Safari World theme park. There were still vast tracts of virgin land that we could explore, but a lot of time was also spent at the crowded entertainment area.

Consequently, when Safari World closed and Game Valley sprang from its ashes, it was new to Jamie. For me, it was returning to my roots; the first days of when the valley was gloriously and boisterously untamed.

The Boy from the Wild

Even bad times such as the snakebites connected me to the land in a way few other boys would understand, let alone experience. For several horrible hours, I was not sure that I would live. Yet that strengthened rather than soured the mystical bond I felt I had with the rich soil of the valley. To viscerally absorb the intense trauma as well as the joy of surviving is like taking a blood oath.

Jamie's worst experiences were more domestic. For example, he was seriously burned when he spilled a kettle of boiling water on his arm. Les Carlisle was again there to save the day and calm things down, just as he had during my first snakebite. It was too far to get Jamie to a hospital so Mum and Les put him in a cold bath and lathered antibacterial ointment as thick as shaving cream on the burns. It worked. He doesn't even have a pucker of a scar today.

Jamie showed how tough he was then, and has done so many times since. He was an exceptionally strong and resilient kid; it's just that being younger he didn't have the opportunities to go out into the bush as much as I did.

Even so, Jamie and I had a lot of fun together. He was a great 'bro' and it was always exciting when he came along with me and Pugga. Mum instructed me to take care of him, and in my way, I did my best. On animal paths I made sure

113

we were travelling downwind to spot anything before it sniffed us, and kept a close watch when he was in the river. But he was a rugged little bugger and didn't need Big Brother watching over him much.

It was an idyllic childhood for both of us. We had all the modern stuff like TV and digital games, but at the same time we were blessed with this huge wild chunk of ancient Africa as our back garden. When we played cowboys and crooks, we could use real bush as battlegrounds, and build real forts with branches and rocks where we took shelter while firing stinging rubber bullets at each other with toy guns.

My half-sister Peta was great to be with as well. She was some years older than me and mainly lived with her mum in England. We all got to know each other better when she left school and came out to work on the reserve for a couple of years while Jamie and I were running wild.

Dad's inherited stepsons, Stephen and Guy, also regularly visited us in Africa and brought tons of fun and laughter to the valley. Stephen's son, Guy-Guy, became one of my best friends, and as recounted earlier, we got into a lot of mischief together.

For blood and age reasons, I was closest to Jamie. We complemented each other perfectly; he was more introverted like my mum, while I took after my dad, both in looks, build and character.

I can't imagine what Karkloof would have been like without having my 'bro' around.

But like most people who lived in the bush, the Meyer clan was not solely a human one. Our family included many animals — and not just the cuddly ones.

We adopted them all. The wild and woolly as well.

Chapter 8

Friends in the wild

T HE GARDEN IN FRONT OF the lodge was an interesting place, as you would expect on a game reserve.

We never knew what 'guests' would arrive. It wasn't unusual to wake up and see a baby elephant outside your window. Or even, as what happened once, finding a rhino in the swimming pool. Or tennis players frantically bolting the court gate in the middle of a game as a buffalo was watching the contest with unnerving interest.

But strangely, one of the creatures I remember most was a crotchety crow that had the temperament of a sumo wrestler

116

nursing a cheap vodka hangover and who regarded the lush real estate around the lodge as its private domain.

Not only did it have a foul disposition, it was also a vicious son-of-a-bitch with a hooked black beak that it used as a rapier. It loved lurking on branches or in the shadows, then launching raids on unsuspecting guests enjoying a meal or a cold beer in the sun. It even went for children, who would run off screaming as the feathered demon came screeching out of the sky.

We called it Kid, but I'm not sure why. I suppose Kid Crow had a Wild West ring to it, and Kid was certainly the most cantankerous gunslinger in the avian world. It would regularly 'hold up' diners with its slashing beak, startling them with its strident squawking that echoed around the valley when it was on a food stealing rampage.

Everyone hated Kid, but we weren't going to kill it or anything like that. It was part of the varied tapestry of life at Game Valley. There was good and there was bad — and in the wild, you have to take both.

On the other end of the spectrum was the most lovable bird you could ever wish to meet. She was an ostrich called Gertrude.

Gertrude didn't consider herself to be an ostrich. She believed she was one of us and our home was hers. She happily walked through any open door, unfortunately leaving regular calling cards on the floor that we had to mop up.

For her, the dinner gong was always ringing and she would readily eat from our hands. She adored us as much as we did her, and she repaid that with interest by regularly dropping off an egg that Dad would have scrambled or as an omelette for breakfast. It was some breakfast all right; an ostrich egg is the equivalent of a couple of dozen chicken eggs.

Gertrude was the only ostrich in Game Valley and as she considered us to be her siblings, Dad decided to get her a mate so she could raise her own family.

He brought in a male, which proved disastrous from the onset. The bird turned out to be the polar extreme of Gertrude. In fact, he made Kid Crow look like Mother Theresa. He was perpetually angry and vicious and charged anyone that got close.

We didn't worry too much initially as we thought the bad attitude male would settle down once he got used to its new surroundings. We also hoped that sweet-natured Gertrude would be a calming influence. Soon they would have a happy feathered family with a healthy brood of ostrich chicks and Gertrude would be an ideal mother.

That didn't happen. One day, in a fit of rage, the male killed Gertrude by chasing her off a cliff. We found her body crumpled on the rocks below. We were stunned. Who would want to kill gentle Gertrude? Besides, males killing females is unusual in the animal kingdom.

We were all pretty distressed at Gertrude's brutal death. She was an integral part of the lodge. She loved being petted and included. We also fed her, hugged her, and basically treated her like you would a much loved pet dog. She was gorgeous.

Dad was as angry as the rest of us and decided that the male needed to be relocated to another reserve as soon as possible.

However, getting hold of the big bird was far easier said than done. This creature was as aggressive as a rabid dog. As capture staff tried to corner him, he suddenly charged my dad, clawing his leg to the bone. An ostrich has a kick like a carthorse and it was a nasty wound.

Rangers eventually had to shoot the vicious bird, rather than risk anyone else being injured.

Killing an animal, even one as nasty as the male ostrich, was against the code of our wildlife management and only done as a last resort. Apart from the unfortunate hippo that escaped the day we opened Safari World, the only animals we shot were warthogs, and that was because there were too many of them for the land to support.

Having said that, we did have a semi-tame warthog that was not as friendly as Gertrude, but still pretty close to us. Her name was Maggie, and she too made the lodge her home, wandering uninvited around the house at will. Hopefully she never suspected that our delicious Sunday roasts were sometimes her family members.

Maggie was never aggressive, but after she had her first litter of babies, she became very protective and would not let guests get too close. She has since passed away, but her legacy lives on. Even today, her descendants can be seen scurrying around the lodge. They have never left.

Another one of my great playmates was the baby elephant Thembi, whose mother had been killed by poachers at The Kruger National Park. To us, it was completely normal to have a young elephant romping on our front lawn, although that was during the Safari World phase when elephant guru Doug Groves was with us.

Everyone adored Thembi. She used to sneak up to the kitchen, put her trunk through the window and steal oranges. When my Mum shouted at her she would run off, squealing with delight.

Thembi was the most even-tempered creature I have ever come across, human or animal. She had two moods; happy and playful, or very happy and playful. We also used to ride her adoptive parents, Cathy, Benny and Abu in the bush with Doug. It was an amazing experience as when you are perched on an elephant, all other animals accept you as part of the natural world and ignore you. They will continue grazing no matter how close up you are, and you are completely safe with dangerous animals such as rhino and buffalo. No sane animal would consider charging an elephant. It's easily the most powerful animal in the bush and could kill a rhino with minimal effort if it wished. Riding an elephant in Africa is a wilderness experience that you cannot replicate as you are in tune with the ancient rhythm of the land. You truly are a part of nature.

Thembi died in Botswana, sadly around the same time that I last visited Africa after having been away for 16 years. She was about 35 years old, which is young for an elephant, but apparently she had some heart problems. Doug and his wife

Sandy were with her when she passed away, as they had been for almost all of her life. I will always miss her.

The animal that had the most impact of all was a nyala calf that came out of the bush one day and for some reason instantly attached herself to me. I named her Gabby.

I first saw the buck from my window. She wasn't a baby, but was too young to fend for herself. I was about seven or eight at the time and I slowly walked up to her. She watched me unblinking, not moving a muscle. She made no attempt to run off.

A nyala is one of the most beautiful of all antelopes, somewhat smaller than a kudu and with curved, rather than twisted, horns. The males are dark brown or slate grey, but with yellow or orange coloured legs that look like socks above their hooves. The equally magnificent females are tan with thin white stripes down their bodies.

At first I thought Gabby was injured as she was bleeding. But that was from a superficial gash and nothing to worry about. The main thing was that she didn't have any broken bones, which in the bush is a certain death sentence. If an animal can't run faster than whatever with fangs is chasing it, its time on this planet can be measured in minutes.

The Boy from the Wild

I touched her and she just looked at me, completely unafraid. I called my mum and we cleaned the cut while the nyala stood still, seemingly at ease. I was convinced she was asking for help.

I then fetched some buck feed and she ate from my hand. Her eyes were focused on me, her lips velvety against my palm. She totally trusted me.

The small creature then followed me home where I gave her more food. I wanted to build up her strength. There was no sign of her mother and I knew Gabby stood little chance on her own in the wild.

For the next few weeks Gabby stayed close to the house and hardly left my side when I came out. She sometimes even followed me inside, leaving a puddle or some droppings on the floor to let us know she was visiting.

We weren't treating her as a pet, but she sure as hell regarded me as her protector. The little doe never ran from me or showed fear. Whenever I returned from school, Gabby would be at the side of the road near our house waiting. She seemed to know the exact time I was coming home.

I would then play with her as she followed me around, nudging my hand for food when she was hungry. We became a bit of a tourist attraction, particularly for people with cameras, and were the 'stars' of quite a few photoshoots.

Bonding with a young wild animal was an intensely enriching experience. There I was, a young child connecting with a creature from the bush at the most personal level possible. I don't know if the bond was because we were roughly the same age in animal years, but for some reason, I became her best friend. Few people have had that special privilege, and believe me, it is something to cherish.

Then one day I came back from school and she wasn't there. That was unusual. The little animal was always waiting for me by the road.

I organised a search party by telling my mum I needed help to find her. We fanned out into the bush as I called for her, my cries of "Gabby, Gabby!" ringing across the valley.

We hadn't gone far when I started to smell death. Something was rotting in the harsh African sun. Everyone looked grim. We suspected the worst. The small nyala may have attached herself specifically to me, but it had captured everyone's heart.

I found the body a few minutes later. She had been killed and partially eaten, probably by a jackal. The saddest thing was that her corpse was barely 200 yards up the hill from where she normally waited for me on the road.

I knelt next to the diminutive body, overcome with grief. I sobbed for hours. But even though I was heartbroken, the tragedy was harshly instructive. For the first time I truly understood the cycle of life and death. I never for one moment blamed the jackal for killing the young doe, knowing it probably had a family to feed. It was doing what it had to do to survive. So although I was inconsolable for several days, even at that tender age I grasped the reality that survival is a cruel business. In the bush, life is a slot on a food chain that can be nasty, brutish and short.

However, understanding that didn't make it any easier. That beautiful young nyala will be a memory that I will take to my grave.

Although Dad loved animals, unlike me he wasn't sentimental about them. He enjoyed watching my intimate connection with Thembi and the young nyala, but he believed animals are meant to be wild and he liked to keep it that way. Human interaction was discouraged, so although he was close, he didn't get too close.

He did however have an African Grey Parrot that he adored and kept in the lodge. It swore like a trooper, and certainly 'enriched' my vocabulary at the time. The guests loved it.

Mum was the complete opposite. She loved interacting with animals and became emotionally attached, as I did. I think it was because she grew up on a farm with lots of horses. Wherever we set up home, she always had pets around, whether it was dogs or cats or birds.

My pets as a young boy, on the other hand, were usually wild rodents such as field mice that I used to catch, rather than domesticated animals such as rabbits or hamsters. I also loved nurturing injured birds or any other sick creature back to health. We had a first-aid boma for animals at the entrance of the reserve, and whenever an ailing creature was brought in, I was there putting out blankets and helping feed it.

For me, this juvenile 'wildlife doctor' stage was purely instinctive. It wasn't as though I understood my father's vision of a game reserve as I was far too young. It was simply that from my earliest years, I related more to animals than people.

However, I only found out how true that was when my father took me on my first animal cull.

As I mentioned earlier, on occasion we had to shoot warthogs to keep numbers at sustainable levels. Culling is a completely different ethos to hunting for trophies or sport, but the end result is the same. An animal gets shot.

My first cull was also my last. Initially, I loved the build-up, sighting rifles and getting kitted out. The adventure, the stalking in the bush, the tactics of stealthily approaching upwind and the endless patience was all new and exciting to me. My dad was an excellent teacher.

We tracked an old warthog that had been evicted from a herd. That's a natural part of nature; when a young boar is strong enough to challenge the alpha male, they have a fight. If the older male loses, he is evicted and the victor inherits the females, which become his harem. He is the new boss.

We always culled the older animals as they were past their prime, would not breed anymore and would soon die in the bush anyway, either from starvation or be killed by leopards which roamed the forests.

When we were within range, the ranger armed with a .22 fired. It was a clean kill. One instant the boar was alive; the next it was down.

A successful kill can be an adrenaline-pumping experience for some youngsters. But as soon as I approached the dead animal, I knew with cold clarity that this was not for me. Seeing the animal lying there with its lifeblood gushing into the earth was devastating. I hated the moment.

Fighting back tears, I was then made to watch staff gut and skin the animal. Dad wanted me to know exactly how the food we eat is prepared, and how an animal that has given its life must be accorded absolute respect — unlike kids today who think steak miraculously appears in polystyrene wrapping.

It was pretty traumatic for someone who was used to having Maggie wandering around the lodge watching a warthog being gutted and skinned. I then knew why my mother never went anywhere near a culling operation. I was so angry with my father for bringing me along that I stormed off home on my own.

My father understood. The next day he took me out into the bush, sat me down under an acacia tree overlooking the plains where we could see buffalo grazing in the distance, and gave me some wonderful advice. He explained why he had put me through the experience, knowing I may find it upsetting, and that how important it was that I understand that in the wild subsistence hunting is an essential aspect of survival. We killed for food the same way a lion kills for itself and its family.

Also, the warthog the ranger had shot had spent its entire life running free and wild. It had lived a far better life than a cow kept in a paddock, waiting to be taken to an abattoir. Or a factory-farmed chicken that is cramped in a tiny cage, never seeing the light of day.

Just as the death of the nyala made me understand the cycle of life, my dad's words made absolute sense. But even so, that experience was enough for me. I have never been on a hunt or cull since, and have no wish ever to do so again.

A few weeks later Dad took me out with a rifle once more. This time was different. He wanted to teach me how to shoot properly.

Knowing how to use a rifle properly is an integral part of being in the bush. Without a weapon, a human is pretty much at the bottom of the food chain. However, at Karkloof, as with almost any other non-hunting reserve, a rifle is used to scare off dangerous animals rather than shoot them.

We had plenty of dangerous animals at Game Valley. But none were fiercer, meaner, or grumpier than a magnificent, massive-horned rhino that ruled the valley.

His name was Big Boy.

Chapter 9

Big Boy

THE STUBBORN ALL-TERRAIN bike refused to start. My father keyed the ignition again. And again. Still the engine wouldn't catch.

We were in trouble.

Big trouble. Barely 20 yards away was Big Boy, coming at us at full sprint. He was one of the meanest rhinos in South Africa and as I looked behind — terrified to the pit of my stomach — he loomed as large as Everest.

My younger brother Jamie and I were on the back of the three-wheeler. If my dad did not get it to start in a nanosecond, we would either be dead or almost so.

Jamie started screaming. I was about to join him when suddenly with a last desperate hit on the ignition the engine roared into life. Dad twisted the throttle and the bike reared up like a bucking horse. Somehow Jamie and I clung on as the spinning tyres gripped the dirt and we were off with Big Boy snorting down our backs.

Cool as ice, Dad sped off, clawing back distance between us and the stampeding juggernaut. After about 100 yards, Dad slowed and looked around. A rhino usually only charges for a short distance. Its aim is to scare you off, and once it is satisfied that you have wisely heeded that advice, it stops.

Not Big Boy. He was no ordinary rhino. He was still coming full tilt at us.

"Go Dad, go!" yelled Jamie.

My dad flicked his wrist on the throttle and sped off for another 50 yards, then again slowed. Big Boy was still coming at us.

"Enough of this, let's go home," Dad said with a smile. We drove up to the lodge. As we got off the bike, legs still a bit shaky, Dad said, "Listen my boys, don't tell Mum about this, okay?"

Whenever he said 'my boys', we knew it was something serious.

We were used to that. Mum worked like a Trojan on the reserve, and had enough to worry about. Hearing that her husband and two sons had almost been flattened — if not gored — by one of the fiercest creatures on the continent was something she would rather not know about.

It had started off harmlessly enough. Dad had taken us out for a spin in the bush and we stopped when we saw Big Boy and the two females. They were a safe distance away and so we got off while Dad inspected a tree that the rhinos used as a scratching post. Their tough hides had rubbed the wood as smooth as a piece of furniture.

It was then that he noticed Big Boy getting edgy. He told us to climb back on the three-wheeler, and we waited. Dad didn't want to start the bike in case the noise goaded Big Boy into charging us.

It didn't matter. He came anyway, as fast as a Ferrari. I remember feeling the earth vibrate as the rhino sped closer and closer, while my dad tried again and again to start the engine.

It was a close call, and would not be my last with the fabulous Karkloof colossus that we called Big Boy.

I earlier referred to the Safari World phase of Karkloof as a Jurassic Park in Africa. Once you grasp that image, you will have no problem picturing Big Boy. He was the T-Rex.

We got him and two females as un-weaned orphaned calves. Without mothers, all three rhinos had regular contact with humans through necessity as we fed them daily, initially by bottle, and took round-the-clock care of them while they grew. But we never knew just how huge Big Boy would grow.

Not only that, he had a horn to match. For those who follow rugby, Big Boy was the Jonah Lomu of the rhino world.

There is always the danger that when you hand-raise wild animals, they lose much of their innate fear of humans. That was the case with Big Boy. Although it is debatable whether he would have feared anything, no matter how he was reared.

He was the rock star of the reserve. The alpha male and king of Karkloof. People came from all over the world to see him. But like many rock stars, he often behaved appallingly.

He regularly charged cars, broke through electric fences, blocked roads, or invaded our garden, forcing us to take refuge inside the lodge. Generally, he was a menace to society. But boy, did we love him.

It started off when he discovered that cars were good scratching posts and he would rub his horn or backside against them, grunting with satisfaction. This didn't do much for the paintwork.

It got worse. One morning three guests woke at the lodge to find their cars had been trampled, one so flat that you could stick a stamp on and post it. This was not great for Dad's insurance premiums.

Then, on a game drive, he once rammed his scimitar-shaped horn through our truck cabin, which seriously spooked my dad and me who were inside at the time.

Dad was now getting worried. This could go south quickly unless some action was taken.

At that time Safari World was at its peak with thousands of people visiting each week. Some would have braais or barbecues for lunch, which is the most popular way of cooking outdoors in South Africa. The problem was that rhinos are natural firefighters in the bush, stomping out blazes whenever they come across them. The smoke of cooking fires sometimes attracted Big Boy, and his menacing bulk lumbering up to the game-proofed visitors' enclosure to put out the flames caused much consternation, not to mention putting some hungry tourists off their lunch.

Another big attraction was guests driving around the reserve marvelling at our abundant wildlife. But with Big Boy now showing a penchant for smashing his considerable bulk into moving objects, Dad had no option but to put a stop to that with immediate effect. Only game drives with experienced rangers, skilled in reading rhino behaviour and how to avoid charges, were permitted.

Even then we had several mock charges and one frightening incident when Big Boy appeared out of nowhere and rammed the back of a game viewing Land Rover. The vehicle wobbled alarmingly, but miraculously did not topple over and the ranger was able to accelerate to safety.

Even if he didn't charge, Big Boy seemed to delight in making us wait before we could pass him on a road. He would be on one side and the other rhinos on the opposite. Take it from me, it's not a good idea to be between him and the other rhinos. So we waited for him to cross over. This could take some time.

Big Boy also loved coming up to the lodge, which was another major headache for us. The lodge was on top of a steep hill overlooking the valley so the only route in was along the road. To keep him out, we erected an electric fence on the eastern section, as high cliffs protected the other sides.

However, Big Boy was one smart beast and somehow worked out a way to beat the electric fence.

We're not exactly sure how he did it. Sometimes we think he just took the pain of an 8,000-volt shock and snapped the wire with his horn, or else he learned how to flick the clasp off the electrified gate. Either way, we would often find him inside the grounds contently chewing up the lush lawn.

On one occasion he broke through the fence and fell into the swimming pool. Showing remarkable presence of mind, he walked underwater to the shallow end and clambered out on the steps.

Whenever he was in the lodge grounds we had to bolt all doors and wait for him to go. Sometimes that took several hours, with all of us cooped up inside until Big Boy deigned to move on. He never seemed in much of a hurry — unless he was charging us, of course.

That's when we knew he was inside the electric fence, of course. He was a master at appearing out of nowhere, and if you ever want to have a heart attack, all you need to do is to walk down to the villas and find Big Boy suddenly blocking your path. This necessitated some nifty footwork in beating a hasty retreat.

Once when I was about nine or 10, I was sleeping in one of the villas when a noise sounding like grass being ripped woke me.

It was Big Boy, feeding just outside my window. I walked out onto the villa's patio, which is about two feet above the ground but had no barrier. That didn't matter as Big Boy was too bulky to jump up onto the patio, or climb the steps.

Rhinos have a unique way of communicating. It sounds like a human hum, and when you first hear it, it's uncannily like someone agreeing with you. As if they're nodding their heads and saying "hmmmm …"

Big Boy looked up, staring at me. I started to hum, and he immediately responded, walking up to me. He was so close I could have rubbed his horn or jumped on his back. I actually get moist-eyed just remembering it as it was such a powerful moment being right next to such a primal force of nature. He and I had both arrived at Karkloof at roughly the same time, so we had grown up together. We had known each other all our lives. We were brothers.

I eventually went and woke Dad as we had other guests and this was a potentially dangerous situation. Everyone was warned to stay inside until Big Boy left.

However, that was not the closest I ever got to Big Boy. In fact, I alone have the honour of being the only person to have jumped on his back.

It wasn't exactly planned. Dad would sometimes allow me take the three-wheeler up to the water tanks at the crest of the hill above the lodge. I loved doing that, dressed in my kiddie's khaki outfit and pretending that I was a supercool ranger.

It was a glorious sight up there as you looked down from the water tanks across the whole Karkloof valley. I got off the bike and had walked about 30 feet when I came up to a big grey rock.

Rather than go around it, I jumped on top.

It suddenly moved. To my intense horror, I realised this was no rock — it was Big Boy having his afternoon nap in the sun. But he was lying at an angle where I couldn't see his head.

As the 'rock' moved, I sprang off as if I had grabbed the lodge's electric fence myself. As agile as an acrobat, Big Boy was on his feet, fortunately looking in the other direction. But he was between me and the bike, so I had to run around him.

As he saw me, he started chasing, but the bike was right there. I got on it and thankfully it started first time. Otherwise I would not be writing this.

I sped off with Big Boy in my dust and didn't look back until I reached the lodge. I jumped off the bike to pull the gate open, terrified that the rhino was still behind me and would also charge Dad and our lodge guests.

For some reason, this time Big Boy didn't continue the life or death chase. As I swung the gate shut, I could see him up on the hill. He was watching me. Or more likely, sniffing me. Rhinos don't have the best eyesight.

I didn't jump on many rocks after that again. Especially ones that were the size of a sleeping rhino.

Despite his cantankerous moods, Big Boy was undoubtedly the biggest attraction on the reserve. He had such a majestic presence; an absolutely stunning specimen whose savage ferocity added to his considerable allure. Whenever a ranger's emergency radio call went out, we held our breath, wondering what Big Boy had been up to.

We had good reason to be worried, as the reality was that Big Boy was a natural-born killer. He even killed one of the females which had recently given birth to his son. Big Boy was resentful as he knew that the young male would one day challenge him, and as a result was extremely aggressive towards the calf. But the female always protected it, as heroic mothers in the wild will do.

One day when the female was on a bridge over the Karkloof River, Big Boy simply head-butted her over the side. She fell 60 feet and was killed instantly.

We were dismayed, but again, this was what happens in the bush. The young male would eventually grow up to be stronger than an ageing Big Boy and depose him as king of his domain. Big Boy was taking care of that right now. But he had to get rid of the mother first.

So yes, we all knew that Big Boy could be problematic, but believed that we just needed to be careful.

Suddenly that all changed. It happened when Big Boy charged Doug Groves, our elephant guru, goring him right in the abdomen. It was the most horrific and bloody incident any of us ever experienced on the reserve.

Doug had an amazing empathy with animals. He could talk intimately to his elephants, and one of the highlights of Safari World was watching him interacting with Abu, Jabu and Thembi. The telepathic empathy, trust and love between them was beautiful to see.

That affinity extended to Big Boy, who also seemed to be close to Doug. Or so we thought. In fact, not long before the fateful day, Big Boy had got tangled up in some fencing wire and Doug had walked up to him and unraveled the steel cable from his leg. Big Boy just stood there, waiting patiently for Doug to free him.

So it seemed that Doug was the one person who had nothing to fear from the massive beast. As a result, he was completely oblivious to any danger while scattering sacks of supplement feed onto the ground for the rhinos when Big Boy charged.

The mayday call went out; Doug had been critically injured. Big Boy has horned him in the gut. It was unlikely Doug would survive.

After a few seconds of shocked silence, the entire reserve sprang into action. Mum and Dad grabbed bandages and whatever medicine and antibiotics they could as they rushed down in a truck to help.

My mother remembers the awful scene well.

"Doug was on the ground, his intestines in a tangle beside him. There was blood everywhere. The rangers managed to chase Big Boy away as James lifted Doug into the back of the bakkie, carefully placing his guts on a plastic sheet.

"I phone Grey's Hospital in Pietermaritzburg to say there was an extreme emergency — a rhino goring.

"The trip must have been absolute agony for Doug, bumping over rocks and potholes in the dirt tracks. But James had no option except to go as fast as he could. Doug's life depended on how quickly James could get him to surgery.

"When we arrived at the hospital, Doug was by some miracle still alive. But only just. The surgeon took James aside and told us to expect the worst. James then phoned Doug's mother in America and advised that she caught the next plane out.

"The doctors managed to get Doug's intestines back into his abdominal cavity and stitch him up. It was intricate surgery and a testament to the incredible skill of the doctors at Grey's. But it was still touch and go whether he would make it.

"Somehow Doug survived the night. His mother arrived the next day. We waited at the hospital with her, silent with worry. Then when he was still alive as the second night fell, we started to breathe easier."

Doug's condition moved from critical to serious. It seemed, miraculously, that he may live.

The surgeon then called Doug's mother aside and asked if Doug had experienced breathing difficulties as a child. She nodded, saying that he couldn't play much sport, but the family never thought much of it.

The doctor smiled. He told her that Doug had an extremely rare heart condition where the aorta and pulmonary arteries, which are joined in a normal heart, were separated by a small gap. In a million to one chance, Big

Boy's horn had pierced perfectly through this gap. A few millimetres either way, he would have been dead.

Doug's mother had never known that. She was as stunned as Doug was when he was told.

This 'deformity' had saved his life. Not to mention the fact that Doug is tougher than elephant hide. The shock of the goring alone would have probably killed a less resilient person.

The doctors removed Doug's spleen and part of his pancreas, and as he would need a long period of recuperation, he decided to leave us. Dad, who loved Doug like a brother, gave him Thembi and Jabu as he knew the young elephants would be bereft without him. They were Doug's family.

Doug eventually recovered fully. Today he lives not only a normal life, but an extremely active one. He and his wife Sandi run the 'Living with Elephants Foundation' in Botswana, which they started with the Karkloof elephants. Abu and Thembi have sadly died, but Jabu, is still with them.

We were privileged to have known Doug and the incredible work that he did with us. He is an amazing man, a genuine icon in wildlife circles

Despite the horror incident, there was never any talk of shooting Big Boy — particularly as far as Doug was concerned. He would never have consented to that. Dad did briefly consider relocating Big Boy to another reserve, but Karkloof was his home. The bottom line was that Big Boy was doing what rhinos do. We cannot judge them by human standards.

Big Boy continued to dominate the landscape at Game Valley for many years, entrancing thousands of people who came from far and wide to see him. His reputation as the meanest horned gunslinger in the valley never diminished.

He eventually died peacefully of old age. His skull and impressive horn is still on display at the lodge's reception hall, a fitting memorial of a colossus.

When I went back to Game Valley 16 years later, I could feel his presence as vividly as the sun on my skin. I could clearly picture him coming out of the bush, snorting and stomping, massive and magnificent. His soul will always be at Karkloof, no matter what happens.

Hamba gahle — go well — my brother.

Dad – once one of the UK's most successful businessmen and
(below left) capturing wildlife in Africa

Dad (bottom left) and Les Carlisle with Dad's helicopter at Klaserie
(above) beating an African drum

Dad, the perfect host serving champagne at Game Valley with
Doug Groves and the elephants behind. (Below) Jamie and I with
rangers on a game drive (left)

The entrance to Safari Park and (below) Maggie our friendly
warthog at the Lodge

Gabbi, the Nyala doe that befriended me and (below) Big Boy with his warthog friends

Mum riding an elephant and (below) the magnificent Karkloof
Falls

Wimbledon – safari style and (below) Gertrude with Dad's
breakfast

Les Carlisle on top of a capture boma, similar to the one we were
using when I was caught in a stampede

Chapter 10

Born to be wild

WITHOUT DOUBT, THE most dangerous activity on the reserve was capturing game. When you're not being bitten by snakes or chased by a hulking rhino called Big Boy, that is.

I suppose that is stating the obvious. Capturing wild animals that can weight up to 1,000lbs and have horns and stomping feet is as perilous to your health as it sounds.

I loved it. You could sniff the adrenaline in the air as peppery as cordite as the pilot strapped himself into the chopper while the beaters got ready to drive the animals in the right direction. All rangers would be on standby — and of course Dad, directing the operation as cool as a General on a battlefield, would be the command and control centre.

We would use a huge mobile capture boma that we herded the animals into. It was hundreds of yards long, and it needed to be as animals often panicked when being corralled. On one tragic occasion we lost a couple zebras unwittingly caught in a buffalo stampede. The zebras were pinned by the charging buffs and trampled to death.

The logistics of planning a game capture are immense. It takes a while to set it up, but you have to do it quickly. The best time is in summer when the breeding season is over. But this means that if something goes wrong — and believe me, it invariably does — you and the animals are stuck out in the scorching heat. So ideally you should start at sunrise.

The most critical decision is always where to run the animals and where to place the capture boma. Using the natural features of the terrain, such as hills and valleys, are essential to a successful capture.

For example, you have to be careful not to herd them too close to the river or a cliff's edge. Or if you pushed them too hard in one direction, they could scatter and get lost in the forest. The beaters — or clappers as we called them — and the helicopter pilot had to be acutely aware of their surroundings at all times while coaxing the animals into a mobile capture boma.

The boma was just a flimsy enclosure of coarse plastic sheeting. It's huge, often more than a quarter of a mile wide and set in stages so that it gets narrower as the animals run deeper into it.

To 'persuade' animals to co-operate, both chopper and clappers make a hell of a racket driving animals into the funnel created by the boma sheeting. The colour of the sheeting has to be sandy to blend in with natural colours of the bush, or else the animals sense something is wrong and veer off. Although any animal, particularly a buffalo, could charge through the flimsy sheeting in a blink, for some reason they don't. They see it as a barrier.

Once the herd is in the boma, a couple of clappers seal the exit. This is one of the most dangerous parts of the entire operation. The clappers have to sprint across hundreds of yards of bush pulling the left and right sides of the plastic boma barrier to close the gap. If the animals suddenly turn and stampede back in the direction they have just come from, the clappers are caught out in the open and in serious danger of being trampled to death.

Fortunately, the herds usually keep moving forward, and once the boma is sealed, the clappers pull the sheeting tighter and tighter towards an obvious exit at the far end. The animals see the exit, sense it is the logical way out, and from there they are funnelled into a single line where they are separated and injected against various diseases, tagged, or herded into trucks.

It's intense, epic stuff. You have to know what you are doing or else risk serious injury.

I was about six or seven years-old when my dad allowed me to go on my first game capture. I initially wanted to fly in the helicopter, but my dad said that was too dangerous. He was speaking from first-hand experience, having survived two crashes at Klaserie. Chopper pilots have to fly at insanely low heights to get the animals moving, and the skills and nerves required are staggering. In any event, Mum would have had a heart attack if she heard I was going up in the chopper.

This time we were after buffalo. To keep our herd disease-free, we had to do regular tests and inoculations to ensure that there were no traces of TB or foot-and-mouth.

I was buzzing with excitement as I watched the helicopter clatter into the sky while the clappers got ready to drive the animals.

Soon the game was on. The helicopter located the herd, flying just 20 yards or so above the ground as it steered the running buffalos towards the mobile boma. Then the clappers began beating their sticks, adding to the rhythmic thumping of the chopper blades. The noise was deafening — it had to be to scare a herd of buffalo. Clappers banging sticks makes a racket like a volley of rifle shots, which certainly has the desired effect. The buffalo started running faster. And faster.

Then suddenly it all went horribly wrong. For some reason the buffalo turned and started coming back towards us, instead of going into the boma.

At the same time a group of warthog charged snorting and squealing out of the bush, absolutely panicked by the thundering hooves of the buffalo.

Within seconds, several people were caught in a pincer movement with stampeding buffalos on one side and darting warthogs on the other.

I was one of them.

To say this gave new impetus to the phrase 'between a rock and a hard place' was an understatement.

Running was the only option, reinforced by my dad's booming voice shouting at me to do exactly that. He was trying to get the rangers to shoot at the warthogs to divert them, but no one nearby had a rifle.

We were sprinting for our lives. It was like the running of the bulls at Pamplona, except even the most aggro Spanish bull is a mewling puppy compared to an angry Cape Buffalo.

Obviously the warthogs were the lesser of two dangers, and that is the option we chose, running in their direction. It still was an extremely hazardous choice as a large razor-tusked boar weighs over 200lbs, and there were probably about 10 coming straight at me. I didn't stop to count. This was no school relay or tag chase; it was a matter of life or death and I knew it.

Then I tripped over an anthill. These rock-hard mounds are the bane of running, or even walking, in the bush and are responsible for more sprained or snapped ankles than anything else.

I fell flat on my face in the dust. I could hear the pounding of hooves behind me. It was all over.

But the clappers, showing remarkable presence of mind, ran directly at the galloping warthogs, banging their sticks furiously to turn the animals away from me. I remember seeing a ranger called Craig barely 20 yards away, arms whirring and making as much noise as he could.

At the last minute the hogs veered off in the other direction. That, at the very least, saved me from serious injury. Possibly even my life.

To understand what it's like to be in the middle of an animal stampede, all you need to do is watch the film 'The Lion King' where the cub Simba is caught in a mass wildebeest charge. All you see is thrashing limbs and all you hear is pounding hooves. That movie triggered a vivid flashback when I watched it nearly two decades after my first game capture. A bit too vivid, in fact. I was sweating in the theatre.

My dad told me afterwards that even if he had a rifle he couldn't have risked shooting as there were too many people rushing around.

It would have been almost impossible to sight on panicked warthogs darting in and out of the savannah.

However, that adventure illustrates just how wild and free we were, unfettered by the shackles of a 'safe' world. We had no idea what bureaucratic 'health and safety' regulations were. Not long afterwards, I was raring to go on the next game capture.

There is no doubt this was an extraordinarily vivid life for an adventurous boy and I revelled in freedoms unheard of for most. This is what my dad also lived for. I was starting to understand that we were not just blood-linked. It was soul DNA.

Every day my senses were heightened. Every day was an adrenaline rush, like a drug. In fact, I even had my first experience of marijuana when I was barely five years old.

Marijuana is called dagga in South Africa and the local strain is more mind-blowing than almost any other narcotic weed. It's the equivalent of 'skunk' today, which is a potent hallucinogenic blended and grown in hothouses. But in South Africa, dagga — also known as Durban Poison — grows wild in the bush.

My best friend Pugga and I used to hang out with three Zulu builders who were working on the Safari World project. Karkloof was politically speaking a separate world from the rest of the South Africa, as I only discovered later. There was no apartheid in our valley; no forced separation of races as experienced in the rest of the country. The fact that my best friend in those days was a Zulu was also something unusual. But at Game Valley, we thought nothing of it.

My dad treated his workers as valued employees with better pay and incentives than most other bosses. Those who worked in the lodge were pretty much part of the family. Every worker was well looked after, with food and his or her own house on the reserve. We never had theft or anything like that because Dad was so respected, not just because he treated staff well, but because of the opportunities he gave them. Anyone who worked at Game Valley learned skills for life and could get employment elsewhere if they left.

In fact, one of his most loyal workers was a man called Skekaan who had been a menial labourer at Hilton when Dad was a schoolboy. Skekaan became a good friend and Dad never forgot him. Forty years later he returned to Hilton and offered Skekaan a decent job. By that stage, Skekaan had hardly any teeth, but he soon became a key character at Game Valley. He always beat the tom-toms to summon guests to dinner and was one of the go-to guys if you needed anything done at the lodge.

So my parents thought nothing of me and Pugga hanging out with a bunch of builders. The Zulu men would sometimes share their food with us, and even allowed a small puff on their hand-rolled smokes.

Except this wasn't tobacco. This was pure Durban Poison dagga, judged by aficionados to be champagne dope.

Dagga is the recreational drug of choice with many rural Zulus as it is cheap and plentiful. It has been a way of life for eons. My parents did not try and do the 'big boss' thing and ban it among staff, except of course during working hours.

It couldn't last, of course. One day Raphael, the lodge barman, saw me smoking it and told my father. I still remember Dad come storming out to the building site, catching me red-handed looking like a juvenile white Bob Marley puffing on a roughly-rolled joint the length of a banana.

I was sent to my room and grounded. Okay, it was only for three hours, and my half-sister Peta eased the pain by sneaking me sweets. But three hours is life imprisonment for a five-year-old.

On the plus side, that experience affected me for the better. I have subsequently had the odd toke of weed and hate it. I hate the sharp taste and pungent stab in my mouth. So in effect, my Zulu friends cured me of any desire for narcotics, even though they introduced me to what hippies regard as the caviar of cannabis.

We also later discovered that our workers had a special plantation of dagga hidden in one of the least likely places on Karkloof — inside the hippo enclosure. Dad often wondered why the gardeners mowing the grass in the enclosure always avoided a certain section. He later discovered that was where grass in the hippie rather than botanical sense was being cultivated. And because it was bang in the hippo enclosure, no one would steal it. Definitely a win-win situation for our workers.

My parents were a lot more relaxed when I started going into the bush with our wildlife manager Les Carlisle. This was far preferable to hanging out with dagga-smoking builders.

Les was burly and bearded, in my mind a mix between Tarzan and Indiana Jones. He was happiest when breathing in the dust of raw Africa, and if Les sensed you had the same passion as he had for this incredible continent, he was the best outdoor teacher you could get.

He took me everywhere on his off-road scrambler while doing game patrols and never tired of showing me the infinite wonders of the wild. As a small kid, I knew before I could read or write what flowers you could use as a soap, how to read animal tracks and what various bird calls meant. He said I was like a sponge, absorbing everything he told me

The fact that Les invited me along on his motorbike safaris is something I treasure to this day. It was a big risk taking a five-year-old up close to a herd of buffalo, and as an experienced man of the bush, Les would not do that lightly. A wrong noise at the wrong time can have potentially fatal consequences.

In fact, he joked that this was his first stab at fatherhood, which I also take as a huge compliment. He now has two grown sons, both of whom are as passionate about wildlife as he is.

Les said many years later that being comfortable with large wild animals came naturally to me.

"Peter's ability to remain calm and quiet was amazing. I used to let the animals come close and he was always relaxed with that. Most kids would be very nervous if they saw buffalo three or four yards away and were just on a flimsy motorbike. But Peter didn't think it was an issue at all. His father's remarkable connection with wildlife had certainly rubbed off onto him."

Les was an absolute stalwart on the reserve. His radio call-sign was 'Seven Zero Les', and if he ever writes a book with that as a title, it will be a bestseller. He was not only the finest head ranger we could ask for, but he could fix just about anything, regularly unblocking drains, repairing motors or pumps — you name it. He even was a medic at times, and on one occasion had to patch up a woman who had been injured in an extremely intimate part of her anatomy while playing on the swings. For Les, that was all in a day's work.

Today Les is a legend in wildlife circles and is the Group Conservation Manager for the international safari tour operators &Beyond. He has survived numerous close calls in the wild, but one of the most painful, he says, was being bitten by a puff adder.

"I was taking some tourists on a game drive and had just caught a big fat puff," he said.

"Most had never seen a dangerous African snake and were crowding around me, snapping photos.

"However, in those pre-digital days, you had to have film in your camera. One guy asked me to pick up the snake again, as his camera hadn't been loaded.

"I had milked its venom a few minutes before, so maybe I was a bit careless. Unthinkingly, I picked the snake up with my left hand, held it while the guy took some photos, and then put it down. But I did so without releasing the head first, which I would've done instinctively if I had been using my right hand. It swivelled like a spring coil and bit me on the finger.

"I was hoping it was a dry bite. No such luck. Within an hour I felt as though red hot wires were being forced into my skin. Even though I had milked it, there was enough residue venom to be excruciatingly painful and I ended up in hospital for almost 24 hours with a very sore and swollen hand."

That did not dampen Les' love affair with snakes. As I mentioned earlier, the effect of his calming presence and knowledge when I was bitten at Safari World was incalculable.

But even so, the realities of the rest of South Africa did sometimes spill over into our piece of Paradise.

This was brutally apparent one weekend when staff told my father that the body of our extremely likable *induna*, or headman, had been found near our main gate.

He had been murdered.

It didn't take long to discover who the chief suspects were. Two Xhosa teenagers working at the reserve had disappeared almost immediately after the killing.

The Xhosas are predominantly concentrated in the south of the country, and there is little tribal animosity between them and the Zulus. Their languages are almost identical. But, with nothing else to go on, initially we thought the murder may have been triggered by clan friction.

Incredibly, the next day the two boys pitched up for work as if nothing was wrong.

Dad went up and asked them straight-out if they had killed the *Induna*. Oh yes, they replied without hesitation. They had been told to do so by the local *sangoma*.

A *sangoma* is a witchdoctor and a powerful figure in most African societies. Few do not believe to some degree in the supernatural power of witchcraft.

In some cases, it is a force for good. But not all. So for a *sangoma* to instruct two youths to commit murder is considered to be a command from the spirits.

My father handed them over to the police. They were released from jail a few weeks later. We never discovered if the *sangoma* had been charged, or even investigated.

Africa can be a harsh continent. But it is still one of the most magnificent.

However, a new era was dawning for me. It was time for boarding school.

For a boy from the wild, this was tantamount to going to jail.

Chapter 11

Stir-crazy in the blackboard jungle

I WENT TO BOARDING SCHOOL at the age of six, mainly because living in the bush meant my parents couldn't do a school run every day.

The abrupt transition was fearsome. From running free in the outdoors, to be sent to a rigid institution where there were strict rules for everything is almost incomprehensible for a young boy to grasp. At Cordwalles Preparatory School, there were rules not only for what you can't do, but for what you can. And if you disobeyed those decrees, discipline was harsh. Usually, you got caned. It was a boys' only establishment and corporal punishment was deeply ingrained in the South African education system in those days.

In the apartheid era, schools were also racially segregated. Despite that, in those bewildering first months, I spoke more to Zulu workers than I did to white kids, most of whom came from urban backgrounds. The Zulus reminded me of home, so I would hang out with gardeners and kitchen staff as it felt more comfortable.

I hated school from the word go. I hated the discipline where you could only speak at given times, the lessons in bleak classrooms, the sterile atmosphere which contrasted starkly to the bustle, warmth and sheer *joie de vivre* that was my world at Karkloof.

The only up-side of the blackboard 'jail' was that I loved sport, where the ethos was that toughness breeds character. We played sport on at least three afternoons a week, and usually matches against other schools on weekends. This was something I soon discovered I was good at, I think primarily because growing up outdoors kept me naturally fit and strong.

One of my earliest school memories was being woken up at 5 a.m. to swim lengths in the pool. It was cold and dark, and not much fun, but it was good mental discipline and made me a more powerful swimmer.

The worst part was the dreary classroom routine, where lessons dragged interminably and I spent most of the time looking out of the widow longing for weekends. I was a fortnightly border and Mum and Dad would pick me up to take me home every second weekend.

I would rip off my uniform and just revel in being out in the wild, even though it was only for a few hours. Being taken back on Sunday evenings to endure another two weeks of endless classroom rigidity was a shock to my system.

But the biggest shock happened three years later when I was 10. We were on a family holiday in England and Mum and Dad told Jamie and me to get into the car.

Dad drove us to the Cranleigh Preparatory in Surrey. This, he said, was our new school.

"From when?" I asked.

"Next month. You boys are now going to go to school in England. It's going to be great."

"But what about you and Mum?"

"We're going back to Game Valley. But we will see you soon when you come out on holiday."

Jamie and I sat stunned in the back of the car. We were speechless. We hadn't even said goodbye to friends back home. In fact, we hadn't even packed properly. We just had our holiday clothes.

I couldn't believe that my home would no longer be the bush. Game Valley would now only be our holiday destination, totalling a couple of months a year. It was so sudden that I battled to process it.

A month later Mum and Dad kissed and hugged us goodbye and left. The new semester classes started the next day.

Mum later told me that Dad had been worried about the political future of apartheid South Africa and had spoken to the head teacher of Cranleigh, who stressed that any further delay would make it difficult for us to adjust to the English education system.

When Dad told my mum about the conversation, she said the choice was a 'no-brainer'.

"We knew PG and Jamie had to start at the beginning of the new semester, or else it would be another year's delay and South African schools were already a year behind England," she said.

"In fact, the head teacher said if the boys did not start right away, it would be better for us to complete our education in South Africa.

"I said to James that the best option was obvious — our boys would get a better education in England."

So Dad had to act fast. The wrench was brutal. It broke his and Mum's hearts as much as it did mine.

In the first months at our new school, Jamie and I were miserable and so homesick the pain was physical in its intensity. The only comfort was that as I absolutely hated boarding school in South Africa, things could not have got much worse.

However, apart from not having my parents nearby which upset us terribly, we soon found that Cranleigh was much more relaxed than Cordwalles. The discipline and conformity was far less harsh. Both Jamie and I were amazed at the easy-going atmosphere, and also that punishments for breaking rules at English schools were benign in comparison to what we were used to. In South Africa, you would get caned for something as trivial as talking in the corridors, whereas in England there was continuous banter and the corridors were anything but silent. There was, of course, discipline at

Cranleigh, but it was nowhere near the draconian level we endured in South Africa.

Looking back, although I generally hated school, I don't for one instant regret being a boarder at such a young age as it defined me. It instilled mental and physical toughness, and also forced me to live in the present. Seeing my parents during holidays made me appreciate them more than I ever realised, because I knew in a few weeks' time, I would be away again. The time spent with my dad, both in the bush on holidays and whenever he came to England, was pure gold. At times I rebelled against him and at times we fought, but I knew everything he did was for our benefit — including boarding school.

He wanted the best for us, and was prepared to do anything to make sure we got it. I knew how hard it was for him to send us away, and that he looked forward to our holidays as much as we did. But unfortunately long periods of separation was the price you paid for living in the South Africa outbacks at the time.

One of the main — in fact only — perks of having been to school in South Africa was that Jamie and I were physically tougher than our English peers. This paid massive dividends in sport, particularly in my case with swimming and rugby.

In England many kids have never been taught to swim properly, not least because of the cold climate. Unless you have access to heated pools, it's not much fun getting wet and miserable. Conversely, in South Africa with its endless sunshine, Jamie and I were in the water all year round. I could float before I could walk, and thought nothing of jumping into fast flowing rivers with snakes and leguaans for company. When not in rivers, I was cavorting in the Indian Ocean surf off Durban before many English kids had dipped a toe in a paddling pool.

Thus it is not surprising that school swimming galas became known as the Meyer Gala as Jamie and I broke virtually every record there was. The school no longer has a pool, so those records stand to this day.

This is not bragging; it's just one of the many advantages of having the God-given privilege of growing up in the wild.

Rugby was another game I loved. I had started playing at Cordwalles, where we often went barefoot as the ground was so hard your studs slipped and crash-tackling opponents was a fact of life. So to come and compete on rain-softened English fields against smaller lads, many of whom had never kicked a ball in anger, was a luxury.

Like my dad, I was a big kid and almost fully grown, height-wise, at 13. In other words, I was 6ft tall and weighed 144lbs when most boys barely tipped the scales at 100 lbs. Consequently, I was unstoppable at junior level. Our team's tactics were basically to get the ball to me and I would sprint for the try line with several opponents dangling from my legs trying to bring me down.

Some of the other schools complained, saying I was a danger on the field to smaller boys. At the time, the weight limit was nine stone, or 126lbs, and the authorities brought in a ruling that I could only play on the wing, and had to a run around rather than at someone. If I defied that, I would be sent off the field.

I still scored a lot of tries, but it ruined me for senior rugby when other players caught up in speed and size. I had been nurtured to run around opponents, not to hurt them, and it was extremely difficult to change to a more aggressive style so vital in the modern game. Also, I was very much a gentle giant and hated hurting anyone. I consequently ended up as a mediocre player, unwilling to smash through defenders, and a far cry from being the unstoppable juggernaut as I was in my early years. The only time I lost my temper was when my best friend was viciously spear-tackled, which could have broken his neck. When the referee wasn't looking, I waded into a scrum and knocked the offender out.

Cricket was another game I loved. I was a fast, if somewhat erratic, bowler and my best figures were seven wickets for 11 runs.

Unfortunately, I was almost as dangerous at junior level as I was on the rugby field. I was clocked bowling at 91 mph as a 13-year-old, and in one game I broke two batsmen's ankles and a guy's hand. But the worst was during a club match for Cranleigh. It was the last over, light was fading and I wanted to wrap the game up. I thundered up and the ball slipped out of my hand, hitting the batsman at full speed on the temple.

He crumpled onto the floor and had a fit, shaking spasmodically as I watched appalled. Then his mother rushed onto the pitch, screaming at me and calling me a freak.

Fortunately, my dad was there and he just hugged me, saying it wasn't my fault. It was an accident.

But I was now tired of hurting people. I was tired of being an intimidating figure. That match, watching a batsman having what seemed to be an epileptic fit, was my last serious cricket appearance. Aggression just wasn't in my nature. Even in rugby when I later tried out for Bath, one of the top league teams, I lost out to youngsters who had more killer-instinct.

My younger brother Jamie was not as fast as me, but he was deadly accurate. I took a lot of wickets with terrified batsmen trying to avoid being hit by the ball, but Jamie out-bowled them. He was soon selected for the Surrey County junior team.

However, being successful at sport did accord you some prestige. This made the transition from South Africa for both Jamie and me much easier and helped us settle down in England.

But my most famous deed at school did not happen on the sports field. It instead showed how cool my dad was.

When I was 13, I told Dad that we were having sex education in class, which was true, but we needed photographic material for a project, which certainly was not. So I convinced him that he should get me a 'girlie magazine' — strictly for research purposes, you understand.

Dad smiled and I have no doubt he knew I was lying as my lips moved. But he also understood juvenile curiosity, so he was very 'father and son' about it. He drove me to Gatwick Airport, which I now know in retrospect was because he didn't want to be seen buying soft porn at the local village café, and got me a Playboy. Playboy was the most upmarket of the sex magazines, compared to Hustler and other more graphic periodicals that left zero to the imagination.

I took the magazine to school and soon was the most popular guy around.

I would charge 50p for a peek and made very good pocket money. I was a prefect at the time, and business was so good that there were always groups of lusty young lads waiting for me and my magazine outside the prefect's room. It was without doubt the after hours' highlight at Cranleigh Prep.

Predictably, rumours started circulating, and I got busted. I was punished by being made to clean the housemaster's silver cutlery for two weeks — but the street cred that I got in exchange was worth every tedious second of polishing those fancy knives and forks.

I then discovered that the housemaster had his own stash of porn, and so on my last day at Prep School, I went to his room and reclaimed my magazine, as well expropriating two of his raunchier Hustlers — once again, strictly for research, you understand.

As you may by now have gathered, my sport and other recreational abilities were in direct contrast to my academic achievements. I was usually at the bottom end of the class. It was the same with Jamie, although he had a far more valid reason as he is dyslexic. He chose to go into the military as a career, and the fact that he has done so well is a testament to his grit and determination.

As Mum and Dad would be in Africa for most of the year, Dad appointed his former Stable Manager Carolyn Boyd to be our legal guardian in England. Carolyn had also worked with Dad at Klaserie Nature Reserve, and right from the beginning has been a huge influence on my life. At Karkloof she was the first to hone my burgeoning swimming skills by urging me to swim 'just one rock further' against the river's current. My life would not have been the same without her.

However, 'guardian' is just a cold legal term. Carolyn was far more than that. In those miserable early days at a new school and in a strange country, she was our surrogate parent, our one link with Africa and knew exactly how homesick we were. She visited us at every possible opportunity, and seldom — if ever — missed a sports match. She even came and watched us play cricket, which was a big ask for an Irishwoman with no love of the game. She used to tell us that it was 'not so bad' as it was summer and she could at least get a tan.

She was an absolute rock; a tower of strength who gave us unconditional support and love. Just seeing her arrive at the school used to cheer me up. The debt I owe her is incalculable.

Jamie and I returned to Game Valley during school holidays, but the exquisite joy of being home was tempered by the nagging knowledge that it was fleeting. I couldn't completely shake off the dread that I would be flying back to England in a few weeks' time. The 11-hour flight back to Heathrow was always harrowing. I would take a window seat and weep silently as we flew north over Africa. I missed the superb weather and beaches, but I missed the bush and the animals even more.

Most of all, I missed my dad; his smile, enthusiasm, sense of adventure and zest for life. When I was in England, he seemed physically so far away, even though spiritually he was always with me.

However, I didn't miss South Africa as a country. Even as a wilderness-savvy but city-naïve teenager, I was aware that the country was being ripped apart at the seams. Apartheid was dying and the death throes were savage. Competing anti-apartheid factions were turning on each other in a vicious internecine conflict that saw people in the townships throwing burning tyres over other people's necks and incinerating them alive. They called it 'necklacing'.

Eventually, the country's first fully-democratic elections were held and Nelson Mandela started to restore political sanity.

However, after years of bitter turmoil, South Africa's recovery was always going to be slow. There was just too much baggage to take on board.

But the really frightening thing was despite the newfound optimism with a man of Mandela's immense stature and charisma at the helm, crime continued to soar, making South Africa one of the most dangerous countries in the world. People were prepared to kill for R100, the equivalent of about £8, in street robberies and hijackings were everyday events. Even Durban, a city I knew well, was unrecognisable within the space of a few years in some areas. From being the Malibu of the southern hemisphere, sections of the beachfront became a nest of squatters, street children and criminals.

We experienced the rocketing crime first-hand when Mum was attacked by a bag-snatcher, although in Pietermaritzburg, not Durban. Fortunately, she was not seriously injured, but was badly shaken up as the crook ran off with her purse.

Out in the country, attacks were also increasing with farmers being shot or hacked to death by criminals knowing that police would be slow to respond in rural areas. Some of those murders were gruesome beyond description.

Game Valley was different. For most people living in the Valley of Heaven, life carried on at its usual tranquil pace. It was a world within a world. For me, concerns of the day were sitting on a rock in the bush and wondering what potentially dangerous creature was either on the other side or slithering below. I was used to protecting myself from what's happening in the wild, and the grimness gripping the rest of the country seemed a galaxy away.

The economic realities, on the other hand, were very much in our galaxy. In fact, they were banging on our front door. The rand continued its death spiral against the pound and dollar. Dad, like most businessmen who had converted foreign currency, lost fortunes virtually overnight.

All of this was happening as I was completing my GCSE exams in England. To celebrate the end of my days at Cranleigh Senior School, Dad said we were going to have the best holiday of our lives in Africa.

I brought my best friend Charlie Röbin out from England. We had first met at Cranleigh Prep School and became inseparable. We did everything together, including playing in the First XV rugby team for two years in a row, and had even shared a few girlfriends. During his final year at Cranleigh Prep, Charlie was Head boy and I was a Prefect. I then went to Cranleigh Senior School and he went to Charter House, but we remained close — in fact he and I were just like Dad and Deneys had been as schoolboys.

When I first met him, I was a foot taller than him. Today that is almost reversed.

It was Charlie's first trip to Africa and he fell in love with it right away. He got the real deal; the full wilderness experience with my dad at the helm. Obviously this is completely different to holidaying in South African cities, but it was the life we knew best and loved.

We landed in Johannesburg and went directly to the Kruger National Park, South Africa's largest and best known game reserve. Kruger is great, about the size of Belgium, but as Dad always said, just because you are in a famous reserve it does not mean you are guaranteed to see animals. You have to go looking. But we would definitely see loads of animals in Karkloof, so it was a risk we were happy to take at Kruger.

The most memorable experience for Charlie was not the usual Big Five of lion, leopard, rhino, elephant and hippo, although we did see all of those.

It was instead at the Skukuza camp where Dad had hired a cottage and we sat at the kitchen table beneath camouflage nets, almost invisible, as we watched the animals around us. The kitchen was outside the cottage, but under a thatch roof with completely open sides.

A troop of vervet monkeys swooped out of the trees to steal food from the table. Charlie and I sat motionless. They were almost on top of us, unable to see through the netting. Charlie was spellbound, amazed that the acrobatic animals had such large teeth and could inflict a nasty bite if provoked.

As they were rampaging through our groceries, we suddenly sprang up.

The monkeys screeched in fright. One jumped so high it hit its head on the roof, much to my satisfaction as it had been busy eating my favorite cereal. It ran out and sat on the grass looking at me and rubbing its head with that 'you got me' look.

Charlie and I rolled over laughing. It was epic. As a teenager from England, this was a story he could dine out on for the rest of his life.

At Karkloof, Charlie saw even more game. Dad always put him on the tracker's seat on the Land Rover's fender to get the best view. The first time we got close to a herd of buffalo, Dad told Charlie they were as docile as cows.

Charlie got off the vehicle — we were downwind so it wasn't a problem — but after a few steps the buffaloes turned and it was pretty apparent even to a town-boy like Charlie that these beasts weighing up to 2,200lbs were not even remotely like cows. He hopped back into the vehicle smartly. Dad hooted with laughter.

Charlie and I often also played tennis on the court at the lodge. Instead of spectators, we usually had several giraffes watching us. Their long necks gave them ringside seats.

This was normal for me, but exquisitely exotic for Charlie and another story to dine out on in the smoke of London.

We also told him that warthogs were just like pigs. Again, not the wisest move, as the next thing I knew he was trying to stroke one of the babies that hung around the lodge. It briefly allowed him to do so, then suddenly charged and knocked him flat. The mother then gave a snort and also came straight at him. If I thought Charlie had shown nifty footwork after discovering buffaloes weren't cows, he rivalled Usain Bolt in fleeing a charging warthog's wrath.

Still, he wasn't quick enough and the warthog butted him, giving him a small graze. Charlie wore that 'injury' with pride, saying to anyone within earshot that he'd had a run-in with a wild animal and had the wound to prove it.

Charlie still says the time he spent at Karkloof was the best holiday of his life, and it was for me as well. My dad really went out of his way to make it special, generously sharing his motherlode of knowledge about the bush, animals and the lore of the African wilderness. Charlie could not have had a better guide.

It must have been a bitter-sweet time for Dad as well. He knew the writing with Game Valley was on the wall. He understood that our time in Africa, as wonderful as it had been, was drawing to a close. The inescapable fact was that with two sons at private schools in England, he had to weigh up his options in a worsening economic situation. To put it in perspective, when he arrived in South Africa, a pound was worth R2.50. When he left the rand was so weak that a pound bought you R18. He lost the equivalent of almost eight times his net assets. It was a huge and financially crippling blow, but Dad knew it had been worth every penny as it had bought so much happiness to us all.

Mum was also urging him to move. She was growing tired of the hard life in the bush, the snakes, the rocketing crime rate and the growing political uncertainty. At her insistence, they were already spending more and more time in England. In fact, Dad even hired a husband and wife team, Molly and Connor Ward, to manage the lodge in his absence. They did a great job.

It was a time of wildly fluctuating emotions in the country; of hope and despair, optimism and uncertainty. For many South Africans it was the start of a bright new dawn, a Rainbow Nation of Africa rising from the bitter ashes of apartheid. But conversely there was a lot of uncertainty, not least being the growing talk of land reparations for displaced communities.

That was one question most white people who lived outside the towns and cities were asking. Would farms and private game reserves be seized by the government? Would the country go the same way as Zimbabwe where illegal land invasions were not only encouraged but actually instigated by Robert Mugabe's government?

If that happened, Dad, who had already lost a fortune, would be left with nothing.

No one knew which way the tumultuous whirlwinds of change were blowing.

There was something else I didn't know. I had no idea that when I stepped on the plane at Johannesburg with Charlie to return to school in England, it would be the last time I touched African soil for 16 long and eventful years.

Chapter 12

The Changing Point

IT DIDN'T TAKE DAD long to sell Karkloof. A reserve of that size and beauty was a magnet for anyone wanting to invest in the bush.

The new owner was a multi-millionaire called Fred Wörner, who had invented the wheelie bin that is used around the world in disposing and recycling rubbish.

However, the final straw in our magnificent African adventure was not solely an economic one. It was also that my grandmother, my dad's Mum who lived in England, was becoming extremely frail. Dad was very close to her and became increasingly worried as her health started to fail. She was in her 90s and being looked after by my Aunt Trish. But it was getting more and more difficult with Nana — as I called her — becoming increasingly bedridden and having to have everything done for her. Aunt Trish was battling to keep it all together.

Like my dad, I was also very close to Nana. She often looked at me, shaking her head in wonder and saying that I was 'my dad born all over again'. She was one of my favourite people. I was going to live with her the time I had threatened to run away from Karkloof as a petulant six-year-old.

She was half blind and deaf but still came to our school galas to cheer for me and Jamie. Whenever I came to her house from boarding school she would put a £5 note on my bed and some sweets.

I was there when she died, sadly not actually with her, as I arrived a few minutes later. I then had to call Dad as he was in America. It was one of the hardest phone calls I have ever made. Dad was distraught.

At her funeral, I read her favorite passage from the bible and it was the first time I saw Dad sob with absolute grief.

Another factor, although on a lesser scale, was that despite his love and deep understanding of Africa, Dad was an

Englishman. Maybe it was time to return to the Meyer ancestral home.

Mum was already spending a lot of time in England as Dad had bought her a coffee shop in Cranleigh called Cromwell's. She had honed her cuisine skills in one of the toughest schools imaginable — running a safari kitchen. That's a pretty serious boot camp for a caterer, and Cromwell's was doing nicely under her control.

In fact, with Dad now in England for longer periods, Cromwell's became a real family business. We all mucked in, as Dad believed that hard work was a core foundation for any business. Even I was called in to serve customers and wash dishes while Dad cleaned the tables and helped our older customers across the road. They adored him, especially when he wore his tight khaki bush shorts and they told him he had 'a lovely bum'.

Working, albeit sporadically, at Cromwell's at times took me back to Africa. It dawned on me that Game Valley had also been a family business, although on a far wider scale. Most inhabitants in Karkloof, both humans and animals, were our extended family. In essence, every venture Dad started was a family business, no matter how vast the income or how big the staff numbers. The family-run property development company started by my grandfather had germinated roots and core values that were generational.

Mum was hugely excited about the new venture and loved England. I think over the years she had grown weary of living in the outbacks, which had been her home for the last 16 years. Dad, of course, never got tired of the bush. That is something I inherited from him and would always stand me in good stead, even when I was living in the cities. If you can look after yourself in the bush, you can do so anywhere.

However, he and Mum sometimes clashed while running Cromwell's as Dad was used to being in charge, and this was definitely Mum's gig. Despite the fact that he was an internationally recognised businessman, Mum knew far more about food and hands-on catering than he did. And Cromwell's was about as hands-on as you could get with customers, your ultimate critics, sitting barely 10 yards away. Looking out from the kitchen, you could see exactly how appreciative or otherwise they were. It was a world removed from Africa, but Mum thrived as she rose to the challenge.

Dad was also involved in another venture, this time in the United States. He was no stranger to the American business scene as he had built golf courses in Florida during his days as a property developer. His new enterprise was something completely different and, at the time, revolutionary: LED lights.

LED technology is a household name now, but in the 1990s when Dad got involved, it was an unknown quantity. The company had been started by his friend and business partner John Fleming, who had initially seen the market potential but needed Dad's business expertise.

It was a gamble investing in uncharted waters, but taking calculated risks was wired in Dad's DNA.

LED lights are brighter, more efficient and use far less battery power. A LED flashlight can last up to two years on one battery. As far as Dad was concerned, this could be a winner.

The first significant contract they secured was installing a railway signal light in Colorado, which led to negotiations to fitting signals for the entire Southern Pacific Railroad network. It would have been massive — almost unthinkably so.

Unfortunately, the contract was too big for a small fledging company and they couldn't deliver on that gargantuan scale.

Dad then knew that although they were on the cusp of a multi-billion-dollar market, they were before their time. So he concentrated on other outlets, such as flashing lights for police cars and ambulances, as well as military use.

But time wasn't on their side. Although they were among the first to spot the market potential, others were hot on their heels. Soon LED companies were cropping up everywhere. Although Dad and John Fleming's company was successful and made decent profits, it was not the fabulously lucrative venture that it could have been. And so nearly was.

Back home in England, things were not that … well, bright. I was about to start my A-levels and Dad decided to take me out of Cranleigh Senior School and send me to Millfield in Somerset, southwest England. It was his old school as South African colleges did not do A-levels, so Dad left Hilton to do his final conversion at Millfield. Jamie was also there.

Millfield is one of the most prestigious schools in England. Among the more varied and famous alumni are former England rugby captain Chris Robshaw, singer Lily Allen and Maha Vajiralongkorn, the current King of Thailand. Another was Osama bin Laden's elder brother Salem, who died in a microlight crash in 1988.

Sadly, I did not do the Meyer name much good at Millfield. In fact, I didn't last too long in my new exclusive surroundings.

It happened after we had won a particularly prestigious rugby game and decided to have some booze before the victory party that had been scheduled later.

As I looked the oldest, I was sent out to buy a bottle of Peach Schnapps, which is lethal as it tastes more like a cool drink than alcohol.

There were three of us and we passed the bottle around, with me taking huge swigs. Soon we were singing karaoke and generally falling about.

We then went to the school bar which allows Sixth Form student two alcoholic drinks on Friday and Saturday nights. I was already tanked-up, so two more beers just added to the fun. After that, we had to go back to the boarding house and one of my friends gave me a pill to calm me down. If I was busted for being drunk, I would have been in deep trouble.

Unfortunately, and unbeknown to me, the pill contained the drug Ecstasy.

That, combined with all the alcohol, knocked me out.

I was rushed to hospital and at one stage flat-lined on the ER table and doctors had to shock me back to life with a defibrillator. It was that serious.

I, of course, remember none of it. When I came around I was in bed and the nurse gave me a phone instructing me to call my mother.

Mum was due to fly off to America to join Dad that day, but instead of heading to the Florida sunshine she had to rush to hospital to see how her seriously hungover son was faring. Unsurprisingly, she was not happy. And once the shock of me almost dying had worn off, she let me know that in no uncertain terms.

So did Dad. But looking back, I think he was not too worried that I was a bit of a hell-raiser. He wasn't exactly a Mother Theresa himself. The wild vibe that thrums in the sinews of swashbucklers such as him is not found in office clerks.

Millfield has a zero tolerance policy towards unauthorised alcohol use. The moment I left my hospital bed, I was expelled. There was no mitigation and I had no excuse for my behaviour.

I took a risk, and I paid the price.

That's also something I have learned. There are consequences for everything. If you can't accept them, you have no right doing them. That is true in both good and bad circumstances.

With my time at Millfield down the drain, I had to finish my A-levels at a cram college. My parents were terribly disappointed that I had squandered my opportunities at one of the best schools in England, and who could blame them? I knew I had let them down appallingly and was genuinely contrite.

Once I had finished A-levels, I joined Mum and Dad in Florida, Dad's headquarters for the LED light business. So despite my parents' disgruntlement, it seemed that my 'punishment' would be flying out to Florida to spend six months on the Atlantic beaches in the sun. I stoically manned-up and accepted it.

The question was what was I going to do next?

Dad, in his infinite wisdom, had a plan.

Chapter 13

Les Roches – A way of Life

THE PLAN WAS THAT I would go to a hotel school. Dad believed I was a natural as I had been brought up in a game lodge that was essentially a five-star hotel in the bush.

For him, it was a logical decision. I was used to a gregarious social environment. As a kid, I often acted as a tour guide to tourists on game drives, pointing out plants and animals and divulging other snippets of bush information. At Game Valley we regularly had high-end corporate clients staying with us and entertaining people was second nature. I have been outgoing for as long as I can remember. Fortunately, I was not cocky — or at least I hope not!

Dad knew that with such a background, hotel management would come intuitively. The core ethos of the hospitality industry — working with people and making them feel welcome — was instilled in my blood almost from birth without me even knowing it.

But I had other plans. I was in Florida at the time, living it up on the beaches having just finished my A-Levels, and had no desire to return to Europe. Instead, I wanted to break into the fashion industry, which was the polar opposite to the macho rangers that I had always associated and identified with. I was, in my opinion, creative and had once designed a dress and showed the sketches to my mum. She was impressed and wanted to know who I had designed it for. For her, I replied.

So instead of hotel school, I told Dad that I wanted to go to the Fashion Institute of Technology in New York.

If Dad was taken aback, he didn't show it. He just shook his head. This was not what his boy was going to do. He was the wisest person I know, and he was adamant that I at least learn the dynamics of the hospitality business from the best. It would give me a bedrock on which to base future career decisions if I decided to go onto other ventures.

We fought about this with intensity. I did not want to get sucked into an industry I didn't believe I would enjoy, and I did not want to leave America.

But Dad knew me so well. If we had remained in Africa, I would have eventually been in charge of Game Valley. So hotel management would have been a natural career path in any event. Why mess with that?

Despite my protests, Dad enrolled me at the Les Roches International School of Hotel Management. Several months later I was on the plane to Switzerland.

I wasn't exactly in a good frame of mind when I landed at Geneva and caught the bus to the Les Roches. That soon changed, as there was a stunning German girl sitting in a seat nearby whom I got chatting to. She was also a student at the hotel school. I suddenly thought … hey, this could be fun.

It sure was. In fact, it took only a couple of weeks for me to realise that yet again, my father had been absolutely right. As I boarded the plane, Dad had said that I would excel in ways I wouldn't even understand, and it was true. I rapidly made friends, and discovered to my astonishment how easy settling in was for me. The academic stuff was tricky, especially languages, but that may have been because I was concentrating more on the gorgeous girl sitting next to me in French classes than I was on lectures.

But I aced the practical side of hotel management. A lot of it was just applying principles that we had instinctively done in Africa. When given a theoretical situation and asked how I would handle it, I would go further, suggesting other ways to add value as Dad had routinely done in Game Valley. That certainly got my lecturers' attention.

There is no doubt that I owe my success at Les Roches to Dad and Africa. Game Valley had subliminally instilled life skills and a hands-on apprenticeship without me having the faintest idea of the priceless legacy I was receiving.

It was almost an unfair advantage, remembering how my father had handled people and marketing, and putting it into use in a lecture hall in Switzerland. I had been gifted with master classes from an absolute maestro without even realising it.

Also, having experienced the freedom and independence of the African wilderness at an early age, coupled with the discipline and hardship of boarding school, I was purely by circumstance one of the most self-reliant students at Les Roches.

My school days were all about sporting success and not much else. My academic achievements were pretty average, and that's putting it kindly. So now actually getting accolades in the classroom was alien to me. I relished it.

In fact, I think everyone except Dad was surprised at how well I did. I was Class President of my year group for three years running and Year President in my final year. I made lifelong friends and networks in a wonderful environment. It provided me with an anchor of steel for whatever would come my way.

The lessons were demanding, but there was non-stop fun afterwards. One of my most unforgettable birthdays was getting the most extraordinary present imaginable. It was an alpine cowbell.

But what was more remarkable was *how* I got it. Cows grazing in the Swiss Alps have bells around their necks so farmers know exactly where the animals are while free-ranging in the mountains.

Fine for the farmers, but not so much for us. Those clanging bells echoing across the peaks and valleys would wake us before five most mornings. After a raucous night of revelry, it was even worse.

Then, two or three days before my birthday, I woke thinking 'something's not quite right'.

It then dawned. It was too quiet. The silence was almost eerie.

The reason was simple; no cowbells were clanging. The hills were alive with the sound of silence, to paraphrase Julie Andrews's song The Sound of Music. (Dad actually knew Julie Andrews — she was a guest at his 21st birthday party).

I soon discovered why. The answer was my birthday present.

Our group of students specialised in holding the coolest, craziest parties on campus, and my birthday was no exception. When celebrations were in full swing, I was told to close my eyes. A cowbell, no doubt 'donated' by the nearest roaming bovine, was draped ceremoniously around my neck. It was my honoured gift.

I later heard that one of my friends called Santiago had masterminded the great Swiss cowbell robbery. He and three other students had 'liberated' four bells from a nearby herd, which would kill two birds with one stone, so to speak. It would solve the problem of finding a mind-blowingly unusual gift for my birthday, and everyone would be able to sleep late after the gargantuan party the next morning.

The farmer was not amused. He wanted his bells back and students were the obvious culprits.

Santiago was the chief suspect, and soon confessed. As I hadn't been in the loop, I was not in any trouble, but Santi sure was. Les Roches is the most prestigious hotel school in the world. They could not turn a blind eye to theft, even though it was essentially a prank. Santi was expelled.

We missed him. But thanks to him, we got some sleep ... for a couple of days.

Another great idea — legal this time — that our year group came up with was the student treasure hunts. Except any resemblance to normal treasure hunts was purely coincidental.

These usually started with barbecues by the pool overlooking the valley below and towering peaks in the distance. It had to be among the most gorgeous setting in the world, although nothing could beat the view of Game Valley from our house in Karkloof. It began as a fun student drinking game, but it soon became an epic event.

The hunt would normally start with participants having to find a certain item of clothing. If you managed to do so, you had to down a shot of tequila or Sambuca; if you didn't, you had to down two and also lose a piece of your own clothing. If you didn't find enough of the required clothing items on the treasure list, you would soon be naked.

Another forfeit was to switch items of clothing. Fine if they fitted, but if not, you might find yourself running around downing tequila with a pair of shorts on one leg.

Les Roches means 'The Rock', and it was very secluded, which was as much by design as circumstance. It meant students had to learn to mix with each other, an invaluable experience as we had young people from at least 60 different countries, ranging from China to Ethiopia. For shy retiring types, this taught people to socialise on a grand scale, and was possibly one of the best preparations for the hospitality industry. Once again, I had a head start on most of the rest of my class as I had grown up fraternising with other cultures in Africa, most notably Zulus. I have my closest childhood friend Pugga to thank for that.

One day, walking in the Alps, a couple of us came across a beautiful hidden lake on a hill overlooking rivers and snow-peaked mountain summits. It was exquisite and we decided it would be an ideal site for a blowout of heroic proportions. This started a tradition; the Lake Parties.

There would always be a roaring bonfire (carefully managed as we didn't want to burn the mountain down), plenty of food and drink and blaring music, usually followed by skinny dipping. At night we would park cars in a half-moon, switch the headlights on and dance until the sun rose.

The lake was strictly off limits to students, so we had to keep these epic bashes under wraps. Only select students were invited and all had to swear that they would never reveal the lake's location. For some reason I was part of the group, consisting mainly of Mexicans, organising these legendary blasts and they soon became known as the Holy Grail of parties at Les Roches. If you got an invite, you had made it.

Another bonus in Switzerland was meeting Sir Roger Moore. He lived nearby in the ski-resort town of Crans-Montana, an A-list celebrity location where people like Cindy Crawford also hung out.

I was chatting to some friends one evening when he walked past, and for some reason I blurted out, "Evening Sir Roger."

He turned, looked at me and smiled. "Your accent doesn't sound as though you're from around here."

"No sir. I'm originally from South Africa but now live in England."

This seemed to interest him and he raised a legendary eyebrow, just as in the Bond movies. We chatted for a bit and two weeks later I bumped into him again. I was playing on a poker machine and had already won 1,500 Swiss Francs.

"Hey, you're doing pretty well. Come and sit at my table and let's have a go," he said.

It wasn't his main table. There you have to put down 10,000 Francs just for a seat. Obviously that was way above my student allowance. Instead, the table he invited me to was a small one for a bit of fun gambling.

We started playing Texas Hold 'em which is a two card hand and five card draw. I played with patience as I didn't have much money, and even managed to con him out of a few moves. He did that same to me. He was a really smart player.

I won quite a bit, then lost some, but thankfully was still up when I cashed in my chips. I was allowed to leave before the end of the game as I was a student and Sir Roger respected that. He was one of the most charming men I have met and exactly as he appears in movies; super-suave and supercool. He doesn't have to act as Bond; he *is* the part.

But what I remember most was that he wore large glasses, so I would be staring at a pair of huge magnified sky-blue eyes in front of me as the cards were dealt.

It was just a small moment, but a wonderful one.

Finally, I was honoured to be chosen by our student group to give the farewell speech at the final ceremony when I graduated. I used the school's slogan 'It's a way of life' as a theme to illustrate how much Les Roches had influenced my life. It wasn't just the education, but also the friendships formed, the bonds forged, the networks created, which was a way of life that would be a lodestar for the rest of our days. I spoke from the heart, and I think it was the first time a student defined what those words actually meant to him or her. I also thanked Clive Taylor, the Campus Director, who was central to our success. Without his support, I don't think any of us would have done as well as we did.

My Mum and Dad were at the graduation. So too was my guardian Carolyn Boyd. I could not have wished for a better

support group. There were a lot of moist eyes in the hall —
Mum, Dad and Carolyn among them.

To top that, some of my best friends were, and indeed still
are, on that rock. We created a distinctive bond, a unique type
of camaraderie, different to anywhere else as we were all
striving for the same goals while living in seclusion on the
mountain. We supported each other and cared for each other.
We made our own way of life, but it fitted in perfectly with
the ethos of the school.

So perhaps it was not surprising that my first job after
graduating was with a company specialising in exclusive
events.

The emphasis was on the word 'exclusive'.

Chapter 14

Glitz, glamour and golf

THE COMPANY WAS CALLED Red Snapper and the hype about 'exclusivity' was not fake. This was the A-team, organising events for the rich, famous and powerful.

I jumped off in the deep end. The first job I did for them was help coordinate a party at Britain's first woman prime minister, Margaret Thatcher's home.

The Iron Lady, as she was known in her days of politics, was a gracious host, although I would not say it was the most exciting party I've been to. Jeremy Clarkson was there and as usual the loudest person in the room. He says and does what he feels like, even at former Prime Minister's parties. I think

John Major, the man who ousted Maggie for the Tory leadership in 1990, also pitched up, so I assume that rift may have healed.

These types of events were our speciality; private, intimate, exclusive, glitzy functions for grand occasions, usually with high profile people as VIPs. I was given free rein to concoct the craziest creative ideas I could think of … such as 'volcanoes' erupting with vodka or champagne.

The second function I helped organise was a memorial occasion attended by the Queen. She shook hands with the staff, and remarked what a great event it had been.

A month later, at another commemorative event, she was again the Guest of Honour. Former Prime Minister Tony Blair was also there, although more in the background. When Her Majesty was introduced to the staff, she said she recognised me from the previous event.

I thanked her for remembering me, and said I hoped this occasion had been as good as the last one. She smiled with a nod, and then I said that I knew her grandson Prince William.

That got her attention. "Oh, how do you know William?" she asked.

"I played water polo against him when I was at Cranleigh and he was at Eton."

"Do you still play?" she asked.

"Not any more. In fact, I still have the imprint of your grandson's elbow on the back of my head," I joked. "When you next see him, please say Peter Meyer says 'hi'."

She had a bit of a giggle about that.

I left the company soon afterwards as the boss and I clashed, but almost immediately landed on my feet getting a job as Conference and Events Manager with the Surrey Downs Golf Course.

The managing director trusted me implicitly and after a month or so gave me virtual carte blanche to run the show. I started implementing my own ideas and soon afterwards was promoted to Food and Beverages Manager.

We had a great team. One thing I learned from my father at Game Valley was to treat the people who work for you well, and also to make the job as much fun as possible. They will repay you with interest if they know you have their backs. So, after one hectic function, I threw an impromptu late-night party as a reward for staff who had made it run so efficiently.

We had a few drinks and then I suggested a buggy race along the golf course. The route would be down a fairway through a copse of trees and back, taking between 5-10 minutes.

Unfortunately, I forgot they were building a new bunker with a lake on the 17th hole. It was pitch black and all I could see while speeding along in the electric buggy was the clubhouse lights in the distance. That was my focus; I had a race to win.

You guessed it. I drove straight into the lake. A couple of guys had to help me pull the buggy out, but there were reeds in the wheels and mud everywhere. We obviously could not return it in that condition, so I left it at the bunker.

I would have been fired on the spot if caught, so the next morning I reported the incident to my boss conveniently omitting some of the more incriminating details. Such as, who had actually taken the buggy.

Instead I said an unknown person must have hijacked it for a joyride and driven into the lake. I 'magnanimously' admitted that it was obviously my fault as I had left the keys in the vehicle. I apologised profusely. Nothing further was said.

After 18 months, my boss left and I didn't get on with his replacement. In any event, I was starting to get itchy feet. It was time to move on.

Fortuitously, as I was considering my future, one of the club members mentioned that he had contacts at the Hilton Hotel Group. He said I was 'wasted' at a golf club, and working at the Hilton would skyrocket my career.

His advice could not have come at a better time. He phoned his contacts, and a few days later I pitched up at the Hilton Hotel in Cobham, Surrey, for an interview. I was hired as a Conference and Events manager the same day.

Basically my role was to manage a team of 60 people that handled events and conferences, as well as the bars and restaurants. I also on occasion managed some private events outside of Hilton where I was in charge of up to 300 staff.

I loved the job, working both at Cobham and later on another project at the Hilton in Portsmouth. This was what I had been trained to do. This is what I was good at. I was at last fulfilling my ambition.

It also was the first time I was doing something that perfectly synchronised my upbringing at Game Valley with my studies at Les Roches. To have the honor of doing it at a prestige brand such as Hilton was massive. It was the culmination of all my life's experiences, even though I was in my early 20s

However, it was still an almost vertical learning curve. In my early years at the Hilton, I was often headstrong and sometimes didn't take advice. I wanted any project I had initiated to be 'mine'. I wanted my own identity. I had to prove my worth through my actions, so I was a bit of a taskmaster.

However, I soon realized that I could do with some expert guidance the first time I had to fire someone. She was 40 and I was 24. Fortunately, before I called her into my office, I took a deep breath. I realized that I needed help to do this properly and tactfully.

I then called my dad.

It was the best thing I did. He guided me beautifully, pointing out that no matter how it was handled, it was going to be awful for the person being fired. He stressed that I should explain why I was firing her as simply as possible, and at the same time highlight her qualities and give encouragement for whatever job she would do in the future. The worst thing would be to belittle her or say she was not good enough. Instead, state there were different expectations, which did not mean she was a failure.

It was good advice, and it went as well as could be expected for someone in her situation. She soon found another job more fitting for her skills.

Five months later I had to do a group firing as we were cutting down in various departments. Some of those about to be made redundant had worked in the hotel for 15 years. I was a rookie but at the same time had big visions, and visions are never compatible with overstaffing and mediocrity.

One of the ideas I worked on was improving our referral systems. Hotels spend hundreds of hours and tons of money negotiating intricate barter deals with tour guides, airline groups and other players in the tourism industry. I thought this was not only time-consuming, but financially inefficient.

Instead, I suggested we focus on the people walking through our doors, and do deals with them rather than operators in other countries. For example, someone who has referred someone else gets credits, such as staying at the hotel for free, or even getting a free flight.

We implemented this in the group and business shot up by 15 per cent in a mere three months. That was huge when you consider that the costs of getting that 15 per cent were negligible compared to the heavily discounted deals we had to hammer out with tour groups and airlines.

I also promoted 'flash sales', where if you book now, you get another deal later. To me, some of the hotels in our group were trying to be Ferraris rather than Toyotas. Ferrari never advertise and only go for select customers. Toyota or Vauxhall, on the other hand, are far more client-driven. And as a result, are far, far richer. My philosophy was don't just try and get the elite market, but rather open your doors with more inclusive incentives. The more people coming into your hotels, the more volume of business you will drive. This will have a domino effect with more people speaking about you, generating word of mouth publicity resulting in increased bookings.

In other words, by dropping prices 20 per cent, you will increase volume by 60 per cent. In turn you will more than double exposure.

Another challenge was persuading people at management level how to impress clients with a personal touch. Some managers don't seem to understand they are in the people business, thinking it is only the frontline staff, receptionists and waiters, who deal with the public. This had been one of the key lessons Dad had taught me at Game Valley: You don't want people to book only once — you want them to come back again and again. This is up to the managers. You first earn their trust by providing good service at good prices, then you reap the rewards with repeat returns. My dad was a genius at that, from personally greeting guests to chatting and mingling with them in the bar after game drives. Everyone who stayed with us knew who my father was, and how much he valued their patronage. That personal touch is what I tried to instill in our managers.

After almost three years at the Hilton in Cobham I started to get itchy feet. Life was great, but I needed a bigger challenge. I was wondering what to do when I heard about an international posting opportunity within the group.

Hilton had just bought out a hotel called the Rose Hall Resort and Spa from the Wyndham chain. They were looking for a Director of Catering. It was in Montego Bay, Jamaica.

Wow. A tropical paradise — that sounded great, so I applied and was instructed to fly to Montego Bay for an interview.

This was definitely going to be a major challenge. My experience was in the Operations Division of hotels, whereas in Jamaica, Director of Catering fell under the Sales Division. I knew that in some areas I would be winging it way out my league, but I was confident my background at both Game Valley and Les Roches would help me land on my feet.

My dad was reluctant for me to go, as he was starting to age a little and liked having me close by in England. Instead it was my guardian, Carolyn Boyd, who encouraged me. She had been a schoolteacher in Jamaica many years ago and loved it. She stressed what a great adventure it would be for me.

It certainly was.

My first headshot for my portfolio

Future 007? Give me a call Hollywood ☺

Doing studio work and below filming in the street. I'm on the far left

I have always felt comfortable in front of the camera. (Below) My portfolio looked a lot better after I hired a professional

Game Valley Lodge, and (below) the view

Swimming with Dad and Carolyn in the Karkloof River (below) returning after 16 years (left) John Jones, Fred Wörner, myself, Tom Baker

Chapter 15

Easy skanking – the Jamaican vibe

I WAS AS EXCITED AS a kid at Christmas to be going to the Caribbean. But it didn't turn out to be the most auspicious start for an aspiring job applicant.

Montego Bay was simmering in bright tropical sunshine when I jetted into the island. In other words, the weather was normal…and I should have known better. Instead, I was dressed for London, wearing a suit and tie and believing I looked pretty spiffy for an interview with one of the most prestigious hotels in the world. After all, this was the Hilton.

Big mistake. I was soon sweating like a pig. The suit was like a sauna, and I noticed to my intense discomfort that everyone else was dressed casually — not quite as though they were going to the beach, but certainly looking a lot cooler than a dude perspiring with a tie around his neck. I was the dripping wet white boy, in more ways than one. I was even carrying a fancy leather binder with nothing in it to appear more 'managerial'. But looking like a corporate toff in Bob Marley territory is not recommended. It's about as non-hip as you can get in Jamaica.

A guy who was the spitting image of Tour de France cyclist Lance Armstrong introduced himself, wearing chinos and an open necked short-sleeved shirt. He was an Irishman called Dermot Connolly, the hotel's General Manager.

We went to his office and spoke for a while as I dripped all over the place. At times I was actually blowing sweat off my face as I tried valiantly to look cool and dignified while answering probing questions about my views on the hotel industry.

Then, to my astonishment, Dermot took me down to the dining room and had me clearing tables and laying out cutlery. I thought I had flown over for an interview for the Director of Catering vacancy; instead I was being put to work as one of the kitchen staff.

However, I was used to that, having done similar work at Game Valley and Cromwell's, my mum's former café in Surrey. Getting down and dirty was nothing new to me, and something my dad always encouraged. I did as I was instructed.

This continued for a couple of days and then Dermot called me into the office. He told me to sit and went to the fridge, pulling out two ice-cold Guinness, his country's national drink. In the Jamaican heat, it slid down my throat like liquid silk.

"You're hired," he said, and lifted his bottle as a toast. Simple as that. I was on board.

Not only did I have a dream job, but as Director of Catering, I was one of the youngest-ever directors in the Hilton Group. I was 26.

No doubt Dermot had wanted to see if pushing me around a little and slaving away in the kitchen would break me. That was the key test, rather than the formal sit-down interview that I had so carefully prepared for

Thus started the steepest business learning curve I ever have had the pleasure of climbing. Dermot was a genius, just like my father. His ideas and creativity left others standing or shaking their heads at his brilliance. I was his protégé, and he was second only to my dad in guiding me to dizzy new heights.

Dermot did things differently, which was one of the reasons for his excellence.

For example, most hotels worked on minimum budget when entertaining clients, seeing how much they could get away with.

Not Dermot. He did the complete opposite. No expenses were spared for valued customers. He wanted people to talk about our events, as that would not only generate word of mouth business, but also stimulate repeat business. He wouldn't just serve champagne; it would be Dom Perignon.

In fact, his approach to clients was identical to my dad's. "If they are bringing in business, you make them gods of the day," was his instruction to me. I didn't need training for that as Dad had already shown me.

Also, he was able to take, not just give, advice. One of my boldest early moves was noticing that the team needed to be restructured. I presented the proposal to Dermot, he nodded and told me to go ahead. When Dermot gives the green light, you know you are on the right track.

I also suggested changing his power point presentation, which basically showed a photo of the hotel and loads of statistics on room numbers and occupancy. His version worked, but didn't hit the ball out of the park. So I redid it completely from scratch and made it purely visual. I argued that all that people in wet England wanted to see was bright sunshine, blue seas and pristine beaches. He agreed, and our already soaring business increased even more.

Rose Hall was a popular wedding venue, but I figured we could do even better. I changed the way our wedding packages were marketed, re-doing our websites to reflect a more visual than verbal approach.

To back this up, I did presentations, mainly in the States and Europe, stressing the romance of the venue. Within a year we had increased weddings significantly, sometimes having up to four a day.

We also had some big-hitting accounts like John Deere and Citibank, and when they held international seminars or shows with us, we made it happen with such glamour and pizazz that they kept coming back.

No other Caribbean hotel was writing business like we were.

On one John Deere site visit we converted a ballroom into a space-age showcase displaying gigantic gleaming tractors capable of bulldozing a hill. A site visit is when clients come to see if the venue is what they want and the John Deere team just said 'wow'. They were completely blown away. Dermot was a genius at taking customer satisfaction to Everest heights.

The 'wow' factor was something I had grown up with at Karkloof. But at Rose Hall I could take it further. The resort had its own private beach overlooking the turquoise magnificence of Montego Bay with waterparks, tennis courts, pools and hot tubs. It was a 500-room tropical playground providing unlimited opportunities to reinvent customer service.

Regular celebrities at the resort included Usher, Lionel Ritchie — a fantastic guy — and Toni Braxton. I sometimes played pool at the Hip Strip in Montego Bay with Lennox Lewis, the British-Jamaican heavyweight boxing champion who got married at the Rose Hall before I arrived.

Another person I got to know was Bob Marley's son Ziggy, who used to hang out at the Irish Bar on the Hip Strip. Ziggy was the spitting image of his father, both in looks and character. He was a good musician, although not in the league of his father. But who is? However, he was one of the best-connected people on the island. If you wanted things to happen, Ziggy was your man.

The resort was also the ideal place to hold corporate functions. I focused on big events and we started to bring in lucrative new deals. It was completely hands-on, and Dermot and I would always be the last people standing at the parties. His energy was Herculean; he was a freak of nature. He would be up all night and still go cycling at 5.30 a.m. He was always the first to start and the last to leave.

I'm lucky as I can drink a lot, despite the hiccup at school that got me expelled. I never seem to get hangovers. This stood me in good stead as I was working a minimum of 11 hours a day on a six-day week.

I was on top of the world, travelling to major cities on promotional drives and publicity gigs, and because I worked in Jamaica my nickname became The White Boy. I was also at least 10 years younger than most other directors. Indeed, most of the other directors had assistants who were older than me.

Jamaica was a huge baptism of fire in learning the sales side of the hotel industry, but Dermot was a superb mentor.

He was without doubt the greatest influence on my professional life after my father.

We worked hard and we partied hard. Even though I was a director, focusing on planning events and travelling the globe promoting them, Dermot would still have me down in the kitchen rolling serviettes, placing cutlery and clearing plates. We worked every part of the hotel, repeatedly testing our systems for excellence. I learned a lot about myself and hard toil in those days. I learned how to push myself to the limits. It was a far cry from England, which is a much lazier and more regulated culture. If you want to go international and be successful, you have to be prepared to do whatever it takes. There are no nanny-state regulations to insulate you. I learned pretty quickly that if you wanted a structured office job, top-level international hotel management is not for you.

I made lifelong friends at Rose Hall, most notably Jaap Van Dam, Director of Food & Beverage and Michael Dannecker, the Executive Head Chef. We not only worked well together, but kept fit playing golf and tennis and I also was close to their kids. Michael made me feel welcome from the first day I arrived. I walked into my apartment, opened the fridge to find it stocked with food, water — and more importantly, Red Stripe Beer. What a legend! I will never forget him and Jaap.

Among my more unusual chores was being Santa Claus at both the Christmases that I was there. We would sometimes have more than 200 kids staying at the resort during December with their families and every staff member went out of their way to make Christmas a great festive occasion.

But what I remember most was I was no Santa from the North Pole. I was the sweating Santa from a steam room. Winter temperatures in Jamaica average above 30 degrees C and there I was wearing a fake woolly beard and a full-bodied outfit stuffed with a pillow to make my belly look big. I was perspiring even more profusely than when I arrived for my interview in a London suit.

I loved Jamaica. Again, I can thank my African upbringing. Having worked with different cultures at Game Valley, I found the Jamaicans easy to get on with. In many ways their outlook on life is similar to the Zulus of my youth. Africa teaches you to be able to speak to anyone. It knocks the arrogance out of you.

It was the same with Jamaica. If you make an effort to speak some of their patois, do the rumba, and generally be cheerful, they will reciprocate in the carefree Caribbean way. They love having fun, and if you do so as well, you'll get on with them. For me, it's the only country in the world where you say it is 'the people' that you remember the most once you have visited. The expression 'ya mon' became an integral part of my vocabulary.

My father always wanted me to be exploring life, and in Jamaica that's exactly what I was doing; jet-setting and enjoying it to the full after just five years in the hotel industry.

When my dad turned 70 I arranged for him and Mum to come and stay at the resort for a few nights. I didn't know it at the time, but it would be the last holiday I'd spend with them.

They flew in from Florida and landed in the early evening. It was already dark, and to make their trip more memorable, I didn't take them straight to the plush five-star resort. Instead, I took them to a local shack house called Scotchies for some authentic Jamaican grub and good vibes.

Scotchies was not by any stretch of the imagination a hipster hangout; it was where you rubbed shoulders with locals in torn baggies, T-shirts and flip-flops.

But you would get the best local cuisine on the island. My mouth still waters when I remember their jerk pork and chicken, washed down with gallons of Red Stripe beer.

We pulled up and Dad and I got out the car. But Mum shook her head. This was too much like the shanty towns in South Africa, which were not safe for white people. She actually thought we were joking when I said this was where we were having dinner. Looking out of the window and seeing colourfully-dressed Jamaicans with dreadlocks and loud reggae music blasting from an overhead speaker didn't ease her fears.

Dad and I wet ourselves laughing, as I had prepped him before about the place. Anyway, Mum eventually agreed to come inside and met Jaap and Mike from the hotel. This was no joint for tourists, but we weren't considered tourists anymore.

Once she relaxed, she enjoyed Scotchies immensely. It was like being in South Africa with the Zulus, just laughing and loving life.

From a shack house restaurant, I moved them into a luxurious suite at Rose Hall with a magnificent ocean view, thanks to Dermot. During the day we would go swimming and Dad was in his element. He loved the ocean, a throwback to his days as a pioneering surfer in Durban. What made it so special was that I could see he was proud of me, the work I was doing and the responsibility I was handling at a young age.

On Dad's actual birthday, I took him and Mum to the best restaurant on the resort. While having a pre-dinner drink, some of the hotel staff, including Dermot, Jaap and Mike and their families arrived to surprise Dad. The party was on!

The meal itself was out of this world. The chef designed special menus for Dad depicting his favorite things in life. There were pictures of E-type Jaguars, beautiful girls, surfers riding giant waves and wild animals from Africa. It was the ultimate personal touch, followed by a gorgeous spread of steak and lobster, and of course, lots of booze.

The evening was purely devoted to Dad and he told us some of his more remarkable adventures. Dad is a brilliant raconteur as he has led such an interesting life and the Rose Hall team adored him. They reciprocated by telling him the most embarrassing stories they could of what I had been getting up to in Jamaica.

It was pure happiness for everyone. When he left the island, Dad gave me the biggest thank-you embrace I had ever had and there were tears in his eyes as he boarded the plane.

Another special guest was my guardian Carolyn, who came over for a visit. It was particularly meaningful for me as Carolyn had been one of the key people encouraging me to take the Jamaican job, so I was eager to show her how well it had worked out.

Those were great times. Life was exciting, vibrant and as fast as a hurricane.

In fact, we did once get hit by a hurricane. This is nothing unusual in Jamaica and the hotel is built to withstand the most severe storm.

Whenever a hurricane starts screaming across the Caribbean, guests who want to leave are ferried to the airport. But many stay for the experience, something they are unlikely to encounter again in their lives. It was completely safe inside the hotel and you could witness nature lashing out at its fiercest through bulletproof windows.

Guest would be taken to the conference rooms below ground when the winds peaked, and staff would be armed with brooms and mops to prevent any flooding. It was absolutely awesome, watching palm trees bending like spaghetti and Montego Bay transformed into a raging maelstrom of spray and foam.

After I had been in Jamaica for two and a half years, Dermot left to manage the super-luxury El Conquistador Resort in Puerto Rico. It was a blow as he and I had worked together like an Olympic tag team, with me feeding off his genius. The guy who replaced him had a totally different operating style and we didn't get on.

In any event, my work visa was also up. I could have had it extended, but with Dermot gone, I started looking around and applied for a job at the Waldorf Astoria in New York, arguably the most famous hotel in the world.

I sailed through the interview stages and things were looking good. But at the very last hurdle, Waldorf's management discovered that my visa to work in America would take too long to process. They needed me to start right away, but Uncle Sam had different ideas. There was no way anyone in the Immigration and Naturalization Service (INS) would speed up my Green Card application, even though the Waldorf wanted me.

Instead, the hotel employed two people for the job that I was going to do on my own.

I was bitterly disappointed. It was like being hit with a sucker punch. The Waldorf would have been the apex of my career at the time, as well as paving the way for my entry into America.

There was another opening with the Rosewood Hotels & Resorts in Saudi Arabia, so I decided to take that.

I left the Caribbean with a heavy heart. To almost have got to the flagship of hotels and then end up in Saudi Arabia wasn't what an ambitious 28-year-old had planned.

But Saudi provided another experience; something that I would never get anywhere else. Unlike the glamour and glitz of Jamaica, I had to learn how to deal with people who had absolute power and were wealthy beyond belief.

I also learned how to live dangerously.

Chapter 16

The years of living dangerously

M Y DECISION TO TAKE A new post in Saudi Arabia was not popular. No-one, including my girlfriend at the time, and especially my family, wanted me to go.

Saudi Arabia is not the most foreigner-friendly country in the world. That's putting it blandly. Public floggings and lengthy jail sentences are routinely meted out for consuming booze or dating local women. Adultery carries the death penalty. Any rule that you are caught flouting comes with a huge risk.

I arrived in the country when it was the most powerful oil producer in the world. It's political and economic clout was staggering. The Royal clan, the House of Saud, was one of the world's richest families and said to have a net worth of $1.4-trillion.

The cultural shock of moving from good vibrations Jamaica to the austere kingdom in the desert was mind-blowing. Once again, I had Africa to thank for my rapid adaption as living in the bush is all about adaptation. You cannot control nature, so you work with what's in front of you. If a dangerous animal is in your path, you wait for it to go, or sneak around making sure it can't pick up your scent. To rant and rave about the inconvenience of a rhino in the way is not only useless, it is moronic.

So I adapted. My new position was an impressive leap up the corporate ladder. My full title was Director of Business Development for Rosewood Hotels & Resorts in Saudi Arabia, looking after the Five Star Plus suite complexes as well as the group's Five Star and Four Star hotels.

The first lesson was grasping just how important Saudi Arabia was to the West at the time. Our hotel clients were all powerful people, politicians and top business brokers, unlike the fun loving tourists and celebrities that I hung out with in Montego Bay. In fact, there is no tourism in Saudi. Instead our guests were more likely to be top trouble-shooters from the Bush and later, Obama administrations; people who basically made global events happen. I also met Prince Andrew, and bizarrely, Osama Bin Laden's son.

Westerners lived in compounds surrounded by heavy security, sometimes with machine guns and tanks parked outside. At times we had to be escorted to work when unrest flared and it was dangerous for Westerners to be on the streets. Al Qaida was pretty active at the time.

News teams were also regular guests at our hotels. I would occasionally escort them around the city to check if traffic was gridlocked in an area because of a police crackdown or Al Qaida bomb threat. If that happened, I would tell reporters we were taking a 'scenic route' to get to their destination, and could not help smiling as they immediately phoned their offices to dictate a breaking story. You would be forgiven for thinking that the reporters had just escaped with their lives, which sometimes made me wonder about what I was reading in the newspapers.

One of our biggest clients was the Saudi government itself. When some department held an event or conference, the Minister concerned would book out an entire complex. When this happened, it was an order, not a request, and we would have to find guests alternative accommodation at our other hotels.

This was particularly true of the Ministry of Defence, the most important Saudi government department. The Defence Minister was the second most powerful man after the king, and usually earmarked to be the country's next leader. On one occasion, armoured vehicles arrived to inform me that we had to clear the hotel for a three-day function. We speedily relocated our guests, while outside were scores of men with AK-47s and dozens of tanks parked in the courtyard.

After the function the Minister called me over and asked for the bill. He opened two briefcases. One was stuffed with a million in U.S. dollar notes, the other with the same amount in Saudi Riyals.

"Which currency do you want?" he asked.

I have never seen a cheque, or even a bill, for $1-million. But I have seen it in cash and it's even more impressive than it sounds. That's the way they rock 'n roll in the desert kingdom. The wealth is unconceivable. Whenever a prince arrived, there would be Bugattis and fleets of gold-plated

Humvees in the car park. It's a world even First World westerners have trouble getting their heads around.

The weirdest situation during my tour of duty was when a prince smuggled a lion into his room in the Five-star complex. There are thousands of Saudi princes with varying degrees of importance, but they all have one thing in common: loads and loads of cash to blow. This prince had booked out an entire floor, and we had strict orders that no staff members were to be allowed in.

What a Saudi prince demands is what he gets, although we had no idea that he had a lion in his room. In hindsight, perhaps we should have got suspicious when room service orders for large slabs of raw meat were phoned through to the kitchen every day.

Unfortunately, one of the cleaners didn't get the 'no staff' memo. He opened the door to one of the rooms and there, to his absolute astonishment, was a lion lying on the bed staring straight at him. The entire room was in chaos, with bedding and linen shredded.

The shocked cleaner, a young man from Bangladesh, took one look at the giant cat, screamed and fainted.

Some other staff members, hearing the scream, came to help. But they fled like startled rabbits when they saw the lion inside. No one was brave enough to rush in and help the cleaner who was still passed out on the floor.

Eventually the Prince was found. He said the lion was tame and assured us it would not be a problem to drag the cleaner, who was still gibbering away incomprehensibly, out of the room.

At least we now knew why there had been so many room service orders for raw meat.

Possibly even more dangerous than Al Qaida bomb threats or lions in your room, was flirting with women. Despite the dire threats of punishment in puritanical Saudi Arabia, a lot of stuff goes on under the radar and there is no shortage of parties where you can meet girls. Booze flows pretty freely in the foreigners' compounds, or Diplomatic Quarters (DQs) as they were known.

Saudi Arabia is a man's world, no question about it. They may not treat their women as equals, but they sure as hell don't want any foreigners fooling around with them. We had to be very careful, particularly as Saudi girls can sometimes be surprisingly forward. At the time Westerners, particularly

Britons and Americans, were highly regarded, and many women considered us as to be a bit of a catch. However, to make advances would be taking the phrase 'dangerous liaisons' to new heights. The Saudis are a law unto themselves. They can do what they like, and you cross them at your peril. The strictest of them all is the religious police, called the Mutaween, who fanatically enforce Sharia law. If you cross them, you could be given an hour to leave the country. Or worse.

However, no laws will prevent humans from being humans. You can drive sexual attraction underground, but you cannot eradicate it.

As a result, flirting took place surreptitiously, such as a woman winking at you through the slits of her burqa as she walks past. I was stunned when that first happened to me as I never thought Saudi girls would be that forthcoming

More common was getting texts. Most people in those days had Blackberry phones, and the trick was to switch on Bluetooth and walk into a restaurant, which would wirelessly connect with other people nearby. On a Blackberry, names would also show up with a message so you could see who's who.

Sometimes a woman would go to the bathroom, lift her burqa, take a photo and send it to you on her phone. If you clicked on the picture, you would connect. These were mainly women from wealthy families who would have several phones, which they changed regularly to hide an electronic trail.

Predictably, I started living dangerously when I began dating an Arab girl. She was Lebanese, rather than Saudi, but the same rules — and penalties — applied.

I met her at an event in the Diplomatic Quarter, which was a neutral zone and where some of the more extreme Saudi laws on socialising were not enforced. It fact, it would have been impossible for me to meet her anywhere else.

Our eyes met and I asked her to dance. I love dancing, and soon discovered she did as well. We hit it off on the dance floor, and soon our relationship started blossoming.

She was gorgeous. She worked as an interior designer, so was more modern, both in dress and manners, than most Saudi women. The saying is big risks get big rewards, and she was absolutely worth it. But her family were traditional and we had to be very careful. We were seldom alone as she always had a driver present. Women are not allowed to drive in Saudi Arabia, but this was not just her chauffeur — he also was a chaperone chosen by her family to keep an eye on her. He and I became good friends, but I always had to be careful about whether or what he was reporting back to her parents.

On the plus side, he would have to remain outside the Diplomatic Quarter when he dropped her off, so even though he knew where she was, he wouldn't know what we got up to. Sometimes we upped the danger level considerably when I drove her back home or to parties or functions. Foreign men are not allowed to drive Arab girls anywhere. If caught by the religious police, I would have been in crater-deep trouble.

So although we were an item in Western terms, we couldn't hold hands in public. We couldn't even go into a restaurant together.

It was indeed a time of living dangerously, possibly intensely so, but for both of us that added to the attraction. She loved the intrigue.

Her family eventually found out, which didn't go down well., even though her mum liked me. I always turned on the charm when I visited, asking her what she was cooking and about her family and other children. She also thought I was

---

going to marry her daughter, so she eventually accepted our relationship, albeit with reluctance. I like to believe that she thought I might even be good for her child.

Unfortunately, this was not the case with her stepfather. He was very religious and did not want any member of his family hooking up with a foreigner. I'm probably lucky he didn't report me to the Saudi police, as that could have caused all sorts of problems. The thing about living dangerously is that you never know what trouble is until you are actually deep in it.

However, more Westerners seemed to get into hot water with alcohol rather than women. Alcohol is banned, but a lot of expats brew their own booze, usually wine or beer, in the compounds. When you see someone loading up with a crate of fruit juice and bags of sugar at the supermarket, you know he's into home brewing. Some also brewed a nasty concoction called sidique, which is basically raw alcohol. You had to be hardcore to drink that stuff, though.

Strangely enough, you cannot get busted for drunk-driving in Saudi as there is no law against it. So you can get rat-faced at a legal function in the Diplomatic Quarter, and then drive to your compound. The logic is that as alcohol is banned, drunk-driving laws are superfluous. If there is alcohol found in the car, that is a different matter and you will be in huge trouble, as one of my friends caught with booze in his car outside a Diplomatic Quarter discovered. He was sentenced to death, but thanks to a high profile father was pardoned. He did, however, spend some awful months behind bars.

Saudi was interesting, but it was a bit of a mixed bag. My moods fluctuated regularly; sometimes I liked it, other times I couldn't wait to get out. I was used to a more open society. Just as I had grown up hating rules as a schoolboy, I found the Saudi rigidity stifling at times. It was this growing frustration that resulted in me leaving hotel management to manage a celebrity comedian.

He was a Korean-Arab and a big name in the Middle East. I first met him in Riyadh when he was staying at our hotel and we got chatting. He told me his career was taking off, but wasn't peaking. He believed he needed some more targeted management and marketing, and I gave him a few ideas. He then asked me to come and work for him in Dubai.

I really wanted to go to Dubai as it is the Las Vegas of the Middle East. It's one of the most vibrant places in the world, where no scheme is too grand and no idea too outrageous. In short, my kind of place. So I took the job.

I soon discovered that although the comedian was a nice guy, it was a mistake having him as a boss.

One of my first tasks was to get him a sponsored Maserati. This was a problem, as Maserati don't sponsor many people, let alone comedians. I said that as he was half Korean, why don't we get a sponsorship contract from Kia? Kia sells millions of cars in the Middle East and the company would fall over itself to sponsor a celebrity of his standing. It would be a meal ticket for the next five years.

He didn't take that well. He said he 'deserved' a Maserati. The irony is that he could have bought a Maserati with his spare change if he had done a deal with Kia. It also would have expanded his fan base in South Korea.

Maserati turned him down as I had warned, but I think he blamed me. After that, we clashed over watches. I got him a contract with a famous Swiss brand, but he said it was not 'elite' enough. Like many exclusive products, the company making the watch he wanted was not in the sponsorship market, so we couldn't do a deal.

We parted ways amicably, and have even met up a couple of times since. I still think this could have been a lucrative venture for both of us, but sadly it was not to be.

My dad had been pretty vociferous about me leaving hotels to manage a comedian, and he was absolutely right. But at the same time, it worked out well for me as I was able to move to Dubai, a city I wanted to live and work in. I ended up living there for two and a half years.

After parting ways with the comedian, I joined JA Hotels in Dubai as Director of Sales for their chain of resorts, which included luxury lodges in the Seychelles and Maldives.

I loved Dubai. It's very western, but you obviously still have to be respectful of their laws and customs. It's part of the United Arab Emirates, and because it is such a high profile city, most people think it's the capital. It isn't; Abu Dhabi is as that's where the country's president, Prince Khalifa lives.

But Dubai is where it all happens. It's the most advanced, most prosperous metropolis in the Middle East with a huge boom in tourism, aviation, real estate and financial services. Oil is one of its lesser industries, unlike most of the rest of the area.

Like Las Vegas, it's partly a fantasy world but also an incredible showpiece of skyscrapers and engineering miracles demonstrating what human ingenuity is capable of creating.

It was an exhilarating time. I was in my element, travelling to exotic locations, overseeing projects in tropical paradises such as the Seychelles, and I had a superb relationship with the company's CEO. Life was great.

Then it all changed.

Chapter 17

My father, my hero

IN OCTOBER, 2013, I FLEW back to England from Dubai for a sales trip. I was eagerly looking forward to seeing Dad again as I had really missed him.

We met up at the Hilton Sky Bar in Park Lane, one of Dad's favourite bars. He was in London for a meeting, but even if he hadn't been in the city at the time, he would have driven up from Devon to see me. I noticed he had lost weight, but he still looked sharp and handsome in his immaculate suit and was in his usual high spirits. So I thought nothing of the fact that he was a lot thinner than I remembered.

Two months later I flew home again for a surprise Christmas visit. Dad had lost even more weight. Not only was he half his normal size, he walked very slowly and seemed to have little energy.

By now the whole family was concerned. Why was he looking so frail? But even though he wasn't looking the picture of health, he still had his indomitable spirit, that zest for life and laughter that defined him. He was not going to let anything spoil our Christmas together.

I took him aside and asked if anything was wrong. He shrugged, saying that he had been to see a doctor who had done some tests. He was still waiting for the results, but otherwise was fine. Dad said that almost casually, as he would never admit to not being well unless he had to. He never wanted to worry anyone.

I was now very worried. I made him promise to let me know the results from the doctor as soon as he got them.

I flew back to Dubai several days later and was driving to my apartment from the airport when Dad phoned.

He asked how my flight was, but I could tell by his voice that something was wrong.

I didn't want to make small talk. "How are you?" I asked.

"It's not good, son."

Dad had cancer of the glands. It was terminal. At the most, he had six months.

Despite the downbeat tone of voice, he was extremely calm and matter of fact. The doctor had said it was Stage Four cancer and there was little they could do. Dad's father had died from stomach cancer, and Dad himself had suffered for many years from aggressive skin cancer. That had spread to the lymph nodes around his body, mutating into a very rare form of the killer disease that doctors couldn't control.

I have always had two morbid fears that have haunted me throughout my life. The first one is of snakes, and with good reason having been bitten twice.

The second was the dread of losing my dad. I often had nightmares dreaming he was dead. I would wake up, my sheets soaked with sweat and would be a total mess for hours afterwards.

Now my worst nightmare had come true, stripped bare in front of me. I have never been hit with such an emotional sucker punch. I felt as though my heart had been ripped out.

I then went into denial. Was the diagnosis correct? Could there be a miracle cure?

I was clutching at straws. Just the way Dad was speaking to me confirmed that this was the final count down.

The doctor said chemotherapy could delay the inevitable by two months at the most, but Dad would not hear of it. He was an exceptionally strong and brave man and decided chemo would do nothing except cost a lot of money. He didn't want to spend his last precious time on earth prolonging pain, not just for him, but especially for his family whom he loved more than life itself.

I said I was coming home right away, but Dad would not hear of it. He did not want me to give up the top job that I had with JA Hotels just for him. He would rather I carried on with my life and my mum agreed, telling me to stay in Dubai.

I shook my head. For me, it was a no brainer. My dad was dying. I could not be anywhere else, except by his side. I didn't want to be anywhere else. There was no way I was not going to spend every last possible second that I could with him. I would never get the chance to do so again.

I went to work the next day and told my bosses what had happened. To their eternal credit, they understood. I packed up, handed over to my successor and two weeks later flew back to England.

I hired a car at Heathrow and drove to Seaton, a beautiful coastal town in the south overlooking Lyme Bay, where Dad and Mum now lived. Dad had always wanted to retire there as he and his family had spent many holidays in Devon when he was a boy. Dad loved walking in the countryside, fishing and enjoying life. It was fitting that his final days were to be near where he grew up in.

He was in bed when I arrived. Mum was out and I walked up the stairs.

"Oh, my boy," he said and held out his arms

We had the longest, hardest embrace I can ever remember.

"What kind of a son would come back for his father? How lucky am I."

I replied that I was even luckier to have him.

Dad said he'd had a wonderful life, and was completely at peace, despite his terminal predicament.

He made that very clear to me; he had no real regrets.

"There is nothing else I could ask for," he said. "I'm blessed to have done all the things I've done and the places I've seen. I'm blessed with a wonderful wife and wonderful children."

He was so calm and thankful at a time when so many others would be freaking out, railing against their misfortune. The courage he was showing will forever be an inspiration.

Somehow I held back tears.

The next few weeks were the hardest, yet most precious and important of my life. I was prepared for dark times, but nothing like this. The fact that I was in the house with him, close by his side, kept me going in my most desperate hours. The fact that I was able to say 'thank you' to him; that my mum, who had been nursing him, could now get some sleep; that I could help him, drive him to places, walk with him, was the biggest possible comfort to me. I had to be with him, for my sake as well as his.

Awful as it was to watch my father die, I would not have had it any other way. I learned to live minute by minute, grabbing each treasured moment as it ticked by. I would stay up at night just to check he was breathing. Sometimes I would hear a deep breath — then silence. I would leap up in terror, thinking the worst…and then air would rattle quietly in his throat again. He was going through so much hell, and yet he was so brave. My respect and love for him in those dreadful weeks was absolute.

We spoke a lot. About everything…life, love and happy memories. Dad was wise…I have learned so many lessons from him. But there was still so much more to learn. I wish I had had more time, more of those golden moments. I wish I had understood and grasped his values, knowledge and beliefs sooner in my own life. He was strict and yet so forgiving. His philosophy is that it's not a mistake unless you make it twice, and that is a code I will always try to live by.

He said he too had learned lessons of life the hard way. He initially hadn't understood the wisdom and opportunities bequeathed to him by his own Dad, and that those lessons were the foundations of his life and his success. I think that's why he was such an incredible father to his children.

As we sat together, with the curtains closing on his life, I realised how stubborn I had been while growing up, but at the same time how reliant I was on him, the person I used to fight the most with. He was always right, but for a long time I never appreciated his magnanimity. He taught me to be polite, to be respectful, to be generous. He taught me lessons that he had actually lived. He taught me to take responsibility for my actions and never blame others. He taught me to be true to myself, not to be scared to do the right thing even if others ridicule you. He taught me to have the courage to face my fears. He taught me true value is in treating others well, not in riches. He taught me that life is a gift never to be squandered.

He had made a fortune as one of London's top businessman, and then lost it when the South African exchange rate crashed. Yet he never complained. Instead, he bequeathed to us something far more precious than material possessions. His gift to his family, through actions and words, was his infinite wisdom and kindness towards others, no matter who they were. His ultimate legacy was showing those left behind that a life well lived is what ultimately counts.

Whenever I messed up, which I'm afraid was often, he never said 'I told you so'. He always had open arms and a hug. He also had a unique way of letting me know when I had done something wrong. I am not good with fiery food and get horrible hiccups if I eat something too hot. So as a boy, if I needed to be told the error of my ways, he would take me to a curry house in Cranleigh. If he ordered a vindaloo, I knew I was in deep trouble. But at the end, if I apologised, he would order the mild curry. That was just the kind of guy he was; teaching serious lessons but having a bit of fun along the way. Those lessons are with me for life.

In fact, I said to Dad that when he went 'up there' — pointing to the sky — he would find out many truths about me that I had never told him.

He just smiled. "My boy, I've done way worse, don't you worry."

I had heard those exact words before. It brought bitter-sweet memories of his immaculate parenting. Once, when I was 12-years-old and started taking an interest in girls, I saw a soft-porn magazine in a shop and tried to sneak it out. The main reason for doing so was that I was too embarrassed to pay for it at the counter as the cashier was a young woman.

Unfortunately, one of the shop assistants caught me and called the police, who phoned my mother.

I was mortified. I mean, what greater cringe is there for a pre-teen than being caught with porn?

The police put me in a van and, with my mother following behind, drove me to the police station where I was charged with theft. They then released me into the care of my parents.

My mother was, understandably, livid as we drove back to Game Valley

"Wait until your father gets home," she said as she banished me to a room in one of the villas.

I sat on the bed cowering. I couldn't even begin to imagine what punishment I would get. Even worse, I knew I deserved it.

I heard my dad's car arrive outside, and then muffled voices as Mum spoke to him.

This was it, I thought. A severe beating and grounded for at least a month — if not for the rest of my life.

I heard footsteps crackling on the gravel pathway towards the villas. They seemed to go on forever. Then the door opened and Dad came in. My head was bowed and I stared at the floor. I didn't look at him. I didn't want to see the expression on his face.

He sat on the bed next to me. Then he put his arms around me.

"My boy," he said. "I've done way worse."

I wept.

I had to appear in court a couple of days later. Dad made sure I was smartly dressed and briefed me on what to say. He knew that this was just some crazy impulsive act by an inquisitive kid, and treated it accordingly. He could be strict as anything when he needed to be, but was always loving and forgiving when he knew I had learned a lesson.

We arrived in court and I braced myself for the worst. At the very least, I would have a criminal record that could haunt me for the rest of my life.

The magistrate listened to the evidence and no doubt took into account my remorse and the fact that my parents who were in court with me were decent upstanding people. He dismissed all charges.

It was a humiliating incident, but we as a family can still joke about it today. For above all, it showed me what true wisdom and forgiveness is all about.

Just thinking of that embarrassing event all those years ago, and how he handled it, reminded me once again of the immeasurable debt I owed him. What could I do to make his final moments happier? I asked if he wanted a trip to Las Vegas or Bora Bora, something he had never done. Or even go back to Africa for a while, but he was so at peace with everything that he just wanted to be with us. Even in his pain, he was happy. As his life ebbed, there was nowhere else he wished to be.

My mum, bless her, was far calmer than I thought she would be in the dire situation. She did everything she could for him. If he couldn't eat some type of food, she would prepare something else. Whatever he liked, whatever made him feel better, she did. She was superb.

One morning Dad called me in and asked me to be strong for Mum. It was largely thanks to her and the 22-year age gap between them that had kept Dad so young at heart — I think that was also why he always seemed so energized. He adored her and always protected and took care of her. Even right at the end, despite his fragility, he made sure everything would be in order so she wouldn't have to deal with anything in her grief. He even planned the funeral schedule to make things easier for us.

I promised I would be strong for her sake. Somehow I managed to keep my promise. I never cried in front of Mum during those days.

In fact, I only really lost it once. Dad was in bed and my mum was out. I broke down sobbing and begged him, 'please don't leave me'.

He hugged me so tightly I could barely breathe, smothered in his warmth.

Those weeks were traumatic beyond description, but there were many beautiful moments. Such as walking on the beach with him and his dog. Thembi was a cross between a Labrador and a Jack Russel, a conception that must have been quite an acrobatic feat, and loved Dad as much as we all did. The last walk Dad, Thembi and I had was a tough one. It was at night, and the wind was blowing, but we went out anyway. I think instinctively Dad knew he would not be doing it again. I had to hold him up in the wind.

After that I walked Thembi on my own. Dad would be in bed or lying on the couch, and I would say, "I'm taking Thembi out. If you're not here when I get back, remember I love you."

He would squeeze my hand as tightly as he could.

He was now getting weaker each day and couldn't speak much. I knew I had had my last full lucid conversation with him, but we had said all we needed to say. We now had mainly silent moments; just a hug or gripping of hands. Every now and again he would give us that special smile. For us, that was enough.

The family visited often and everyone tried to be as strong as they could. Jamie, Peta and Stephen, Dad's stepson, came down whenever possible. Peta took it exceptionally hard as she adored Dad, while his other stepson, Guy made a surprise trip from Australia. It was an incredible moment for Dad that his stepson had come from so far to say how much he loved him. When Guy left to go home, he knew it would be the last time he would see Dad. It was a heart-breaking farewell.

The final week was the most brutal in my life. Mum and I never knew if he was drawing his last breath. I spent most nights in his room with a blanket around me, just watching him.

As death started closing in, we had to increase his morphine dose. Dad was an incredibly tough guy and only switched to morphine right at the end when the pain got too bad. His courage was like granite. He didn't want any other support except his immediate family. He didn't want a hospital bed and intravenous drips sticking out of his arms. He wanted to be at home with the people he loved. He wanted to die in his own bed.

It was a little past 10 on the morning of March 4, 2014 when the end came.

My mother and I were holding his hands. Mum whispered to him, "It's okay, you can go," she said.

I could feel his pulse. It was barely throbbing.

Then he was gone.

Both Mum and I heard his last breath.

His grip on my hand softened.

I can still feel it to this day.

The doctor told us to let Thembi smell Dad the moment he passed, so we brought her to the bed. It was wonderful to watch. She sniffed him intently for several seconds, all over his body, then gave him a little lick on his cheek. From there she went and sat next to Mum, as if to comfort her. Or perhaps to be comforted. She knew Dad had gone. It was incredible. I have never seen anything like it.

Mum and I washed Dad and dressed him in his smart clothes and his favorite green South African rugby jacket, the team he supported, even though he was an Englishman.

He always was a gentleman and liked to look his best. We were not going to change that now.

The driver from the morgue arrived to take Dad away. Mum was understandably too emotional to watch Dad go, so I handled it.

He looked so peaceful on the bed, dressed so smart and comfortable and still handsome as ever.

It was the last time I saw him.

I have never felt so alone, and in some ways it was the first time I felt truly vulnerable. No-one really knows loss until they lose a parent. That bubble of protection is gone in an instant.

Seeing the greatest part of my life die in my arms was the worst thing ever. Everything that had really made me and made me whole was gone. That moment hit me hard. But it was so precious to be there at the last moments with the person who brought me into this world — to help take him out.

Chapter 18

The funeral

I HAD VOWED TO DAD on his death bed that I would keep it all together for Mum. I promised I would not break down.

So far I had kept my word. But the final and harshest test would be the actual funeral.

I wasn't sure whether I could pull it off. My grief was overwhelming, as was the rest of the family's. All I knew was that I had to do him proud.

What made it even more melancholic was that our entire family had been engulfed by death and sadness for the past few months. Firstly, my aunt Trish Tucker, Dad's sister, passed away several weeks before he did, also from cancer. Trish's wake was made more poignant for us as it was held at the Hurtwood Park Polo Club, the same venue where Dad's wake was scheduled to be held. However, Dad was completely at peace during the service, as if he knew he would be seeing her again soon.

Soon after that, Dad's exceptionally close cousin, Grant Wilkinson died. Grant had been instrumental in encouraging Dad to marry Mum, despite their age difference. His reasoning was simple: they loved each other

Then one of Mum's aunts, Moyra died. Mum's best friend and her best friend's mother also were killed in a car crash, bringing the death toll of family and friends to five in a few short months.

It was a bleak time for everyone, culminating in the biggest sorrow of all; Dad's death.

His funeral was scheduled to be held in 10 days' time. It was to be a cremation attended by close friends and family, followed by a traditional ceremony with a church service. Then, finally, a wake in his honour.

I was staying with my best friend Charlie Röbin. Since my schooldays, the Röbins have been my second family and

Charlie's fantastic folks Tony and Julia — who call me Pedro — have always treated me as a son. I was the Best Man at Charlie and Sarah's wedding, and they did me the ultimate honour of asking me to be Godfather to their daughter Evelyn. I could not have had a better support system to get me through the day.

I woke that morning in a complete state. I was an absolute emotional wreck. I couldn't knot my tie or fix my cufflinks. I could barely tie my shoelaces. Charlie practically dressed me. A wonderful, wonderful friend.

My brother Jamie, Dad's stepsons Guy and Stephen, my mum's brother Grant, and Charlie Röbin were my fellow pallbearers. I was at the front of the coffin with Guy and we lifted Dad's coffin onto our shoulders. At that instant, I knew exactly what the saying the 'weight of the world on your shoulders' truly meant.

When we arrived at the church, it was bursting at the seams. The pews were overflowing. There must have been about 250 people from around the country. We never expected such a massive turnout, and judging by the apologies and condolences we received, at least 500 people were with us in spirit. It was magnificent, although highly emotional, to see so many people coming to pay tribute to a man who had obviously touched their lives.

The church itself was symbolic as it had been a huge part of Dad's life. Whenever possible, he had attended Sunday services there. His mother had died in the Old Rectory Nursing Home right next door to it, and her funeral service had been held there as well.

From the church, mourners went to the Hurtwood Polo Club for a final toast to Dad. He had loved the club and had spent many years walking the fields with his faithful dog Thembi. The two houses that we had lived in before Dad retired to Devon where on different sides of the club, so it also had great sentimental value.

There were tears and laughter wherever you looked. Tears for the loss; laughter for the joy that Dad had brought so many. There were some lovely readings, some hilarious reminiscences, and all in all it was a wonderful day. I looked at the sky. I knew my father was smiling up there, with us in spirit and enjoying the party as well.

Mum was bowled over by the number of people who had come to pay their respects. She had incredible love and support that day from everyone, especially her sister Julie, who was an absolute pillar of strength. Mum was staying with Julie, and having her family around, cooking, organizing and having a shoulder to cry on whenever needed, was a massive comfort to her. Julie's devoted support also allowed me to have some time to myself and prepare for the funeral. I've always had a soft spot for my Aunt Julie as she is such a warm, generous person. When I was at Les Roches, she once caught the train from Amsterdam and came all the way to Switzerland just to give me a TV set for my room.

Mum was remarkably strong at the funeral and I was proud of her. I spent some time comforting her as she had just lost the love of her life. I knew her grief was tempered with gratitude that she had shared so much with such an exceptional person.

"Your dad was incredible," she said to me. "Whatever he put his mind to, he could do so well. You just couldn't say no to him. He was irrepressible, a true force of nature."

Les Carlisle, the ranger who had worked closely with Dad at both Klaserie and Karkloof, sadly couldn't make it to the funeral. We tried to get him over from Africa, but the timing was just not right. Anyway, we knew how much he and Dad meant to each other and always would.

In his absence, Les sent us a eulogy that he asked to be read out if possible. It was a simple, heartfelt piece that was …well, so marvelously 'Les'.

"You all must know that Jimmy had a profound influence in our lives and many other people's lives too.

Jimmy was and will always be a role model, a giver, a man to be followed.

He flew into our lives, literally in a helicopter, and before we knew it he was flying full time for the game capture unit, and in a turbine helicopter.

Jimmy imported the first 500 E helicopter, into country when we were still looking at them in magazines. I remember the reason for the import was a crash in the red and white 500 C helicopter. Jimmy was lying on a stainless steel table with a gaping gash in his head, Dr. Blackie Swart said, with his stern face, that he can see right into Jimmy's brain, and he is a little worried … as there is nothing there!

The focus that Jimmy brought to bush clearing, using forestry machines changed the way people tackle bush

278

encroachment completely and permanently. The commitment and passion that Jimmy did everything in life with, was never more evident than when he took on the task of turning a beautiful cattle farming valley into a spectacular game reserve. A developer at heart, the Karkloof Falls Game reserve grew out of his vision and passion. Hundreds of people shared the incredible experience both as day visitors and in the beautifully crafted Fish Eagle Camp with great Narina Trogon viewing.

The Honeymoon Suite nestled against the forest edge provided great viewing of the elusive Green Twinspot, and a glimpse of heaven, that Jimmy is no doubt influencing now.

The redevelopment of Game Valley after the floods had washed Fish Eagle camp into Albert Falls Dam was driven by a desire to share this exquisite piece of heaven with as many people and especially disadvantaged children as he could. Thousands of school kids and families were exposed to wildlife by this unselfish drive to make wildlife accessible to all. This was ground breaking in the South Africa of late 1980s.

Jimmy believed that the leaders of the future were the children and they needed access to the wildlife of the country.

They certainly couldn't get to the big game reserves from Pietermaritzburg in any sort of numbers.

The Karkloof and Umgeni Valley are combined today in one big game reserve that stands as a monument to Jimmy's vision.

So Mandy, PG and Jamie, I hope the Lord is ready, as Jimmy will be developing heaven, to make it accessible to more people. That is Jimmy's way!

Les, Lynette, Damian and Dean Carlisle

The time came for my eulogy. The hardest thing for me was to keep my roller-coasting emotions in check. I could not allow myself the luxury of weeping. I had promised Dad that. I may have had to grow up quickly as a child in the bush and being sent to boarding school so young, but I believe I truly became a man that day.

I looked at the sea of faces in front of me, and suddenly I felt calm.

It was such a beautiful, rather than sorrowful, sight as I vividly saw how much love there was for a man, my father, who had warmed the lives of so many people.

Dad had written some words for me, but when I told him I had already prepared something, I gave it to him to read.

He tore up his piece. He wanted me to read mine.

My Father, a Lighthouse

I have been thinking how best to describe you to others and myself but also those whom you sadly won't meet. What man could I relate to you, then I realize there isn't anyone in this world like you. Especially a man who can tackle an Ostrich or face a Rhino or ride away on a 3-wheeler bike with Jamie and myself on the back while being chased by the Rhino known as Big Boy (Mum, he had said we were not to tell you back then).

Or even fly a helicopter in harsh conditions and crash-land among 300 Buffalo in the middle of nowhere in Africa and still live to tell the tale. Or even the man to cycle to work in the middle of winter in only your purple safari shorts, of which the older grannies of Cranleigh would wake up to every day just to get a glimpse out the window at you and your 'sexy bum', as most would say. It was the highlight of their day. You are a man of greatness and so unique, the only of your

281

kind, so I can't think of any man to compare, not even your father.

Maybe an animal but then you prey on nothing and are hunted by none, pure perfection by any creature God created.

Besides, you had a safari park with all the animals and were the ruler of them all. You were even able to tame the wildest of them all, (well actually Mum you are still pretty hard to handle so we will still keep the cage just in case).

Maybe a star shining bright, but then again you are better than all of them and symbolize so much more. Not even a Hollywood Star has what you have Dad. Even Patrick Swayze, who looked like you, didn't even have your dance moves.

What could define my dearest father, and then it hit me, like a lightning bolt and maybe it was Nana telling me because there was a painting she had and it reminds me of you. There was a lady and a little boy playing by the sea and I always felt it was you and Nana. It was beautiful and stunning, but in the background there was something that was always there that never seemed to make the image what it was until now, and this is why what I feel outlines you perfectly.

You are like a Lighthouse, and here's why:

You stand tall and proud, glorious and gorgeous. You are the beacon of hope and perfection that is not designed to be admired for just its beauty, but for the natural goodness you are and the purpose you serve and those whom you touch. You are strong and tough and able to handle anything yet still be soft, able to look after and care for others. Even if aged, you are still magnificent, handsome and beautiful with style and grace.

You overlook us, you are there for us and you protect us. You put yourself there to save us through the storms even if you take the hits yourself. You guide us and warn us about all the dangers ahead. You become a shelter even when it feels like the world is falling down on you. And even when the storms are at its worst and you feel you have hit a low, you still manage to stand tall and stay strong, you rub off and hide your bruises and even on your last legs you still remain there to help everyone else but yourself.

But even through all that, the biggest thing is this, your light …. Your light is forever bright and shining far and wide for us all. Your light makes us smile, makes us joyful and has made us so happy and safe. Your light has guided us and always shown us the way. Your light shines so far that it has helped even those not around you. Your presence has affected those who you have not even met or seen but know you are there and what you represent and how you have affected so many lives. Your light is quite simply this; it is love … and it is so pure. You are there and shine for all yet you ask for nothing in return but our happiness, safety and ability to live life freely and joyfully and pass through any storm if we have to and handle it or even in some cases you allow us not to even have the storm fall upon us.

You, like the lighthouse, are completely Selfless and only have served to give to others and have never taken.

You are the only Wonder of the World, for you are there as a purpose, a symbol, a masterpiece of utter delight, beauty and perfection. You are there for the world but especially those closest around you.

You may not be with us anymore Dad but your light will forever shine upon us.

On his tombstone is this simple tribute: Beloved Husband, Father, Friend. Forever Young.

Chapter 19

Life after Dad

A FTER THE FUNERAL, I stayed in England for several months to support my mum and help her recover her full emotional strength.

I could now also finally start to grieve. And I did, from the depths of my soul. The emptiness that Dad left behind was so intense that I felt truly alone for the first time. He had been so wonderful, so inspirational, that it was difficult to grasp the reality that he was no longer physically with me.

He was in spirit, of course, and will be so every minute for the rest of my life.

It was a terrible time for all of us. Today I still cannot see a hearse driving on the road without getting a lump in my throat.

However, I needed to get back to work. A dream job soon came up as Director of Sales and Marketing for the YTL Hotel group based in Kuala Lumpur, Malaysia. I applied and was accepted.

On paper it was the perfect position. I had a gigantic role with a big salary and perks that included a penthouse and good prospects of promotion in a rapidly growing company. My area of operations was Malaysia, Bali, Thailand and Japan — a huge and influential chunk of Asia.

It should have been exactly the medicine I needed. A stimulating and challenging career to make a new start in life, now that my father, mentor, best friend, confidant, advisor and absolute hero was no longer here.

But it wasn't. It was almost the exact opposite. My mind was simply not in the right place. The job at YTL was high profile and intense and there was no doubt that I could do whatever was required of me, thanks to my experience and upbringing. There was nothing I could not handle, as I had been trained by the best in the industry.

But there was one crucial difference. I no longer had Dad's guidance. I could no longer speed dial him for advice or a plan of action. Or even just to hear him say "my boy".

I left after six months and returned to England. Even though YTL were happy with me, I didn't feel as though I was giving the job my best shot due to my bottomless grief.

I now had to face up to reality; what exactly did I want to do with my life? Where was I going? Did I really want to stay in the hotel industry?

That was probably the key question. The hospitality business was something I had been born into and so far I had been successful. Becoming one of the youngest-ever directors at the Hilton group — of which there are more than 3,000 hotels — was something I'll always be proud of. I was confident that I would do a good job if I went back into the industry, but my stint in Malaysia made me question if my heart was still in it. Did I still have the passion? Dad always did everything with passion, and I am the same. If there is no flame, there is no point.

I thought about that long and hard. If I was being true to myself, the answer would have been 'no'. The passion was gone. The flame was burning low. At least at that time. It may return later, but I needed a clean break and do something not only new, but totally off the wall.

In hindsight, that was exactly what my father had done many years ago. He had reached the pinnacle of business, he was the James Dean of the commercial world…then he packed it up and started a game reserve in Africa.

When I was younger I had done some modelling to make money on the side. I was always up for earning extra cash, and had once moonlighted as a lifesaver while my parents believed I was swotting for my school GCSE exams. In other words, I was eyeing pretty girls in bikinis while they thought I was nose-deep in books, which kind of is the story of my schooldays.

I had no intention of becoming a lifesaver…but why not try out modelling again? The short stint I had earlier done had been good. Maybe I should consider doing something similar along those lines.

As fate would have it, one of our closest family friends, Wendy Hancock, had come up from South Africa for Dad's funeral. We spent many hours chatting. She is a quality person and I've been fortunate to have forged a special bond with her since she worked with us at Karkloof.

I mentioned to Wendy that I needed to do something new, and she was the perfect person to confide in. She had taken me for my first portfolio shoot in London some years back, just before I left for Les Roches in Switzerland, and had remarked that I was very comfortable in front of the camera. Wendy told me she believed that I had the passion to make it in the fickle world of fashion.

Passion was the exact word I was looking for. It was what I wanted to hear.

Wendy suggested I start off by registering on StarNow, which is an online platform for the entertainment industry. Three days later I got a direct call from a production company called GForces saying I had the 'perfect look' for a car commercial. I hadn't even applied for the job.

I arrived at the studio in the morning. We got the shoot done in a single take. The director, Martin Bean was impressed.

"Hey, you're a natural," he said.

I was amazed. "But all I had to do was open a car door and smile," I said.

"Yeah, but some people don't even have the confidence to do that on their own. They need a lot of direction. You don't."

Martin said I should consider doing some acting as well, which would significantly add to my marketability. As soon as I got home, I followed his advice and went online to apply for more gigs.

Not long afterwards I got a call from a film director, who contacted me directly for a TV News Anchor role for an independent British film. It wasn't a paid job, but I would be given a credit, which basically means I would get an industry endorsement. I could have immediately said no, as I needed the money. But I thought about it, then decided that a credit at that stage of my fledging career would possibly be worth more than payment as agencies want to see what work you have done. It would look great on my résumé.

I agreed without hesitation.

I had to drive all the way to Norwich and it cost me about £80 out of my own pocket. Not only was there no payment involved, I couldn't claim for expenses either. I had no idea what I was letting myself in for, but at the very least, I told myself it would be a cool adventure. I love doing new stuff.

At the studio I quickly went over my lines and, like the car commercial, nailed the shoot on the first take. That got the director's attention. Would I mind trying it in another style?

No problem — again, it took only one take.

We hung around for a bit, then the director came up to me again.

"The other actor hasn't pitched up. Would you mind doing his lines as well?"

No problem. They gave me the script and while I was outside rehearsing, I realised how much I was enjoying myself. I knew at that instant this was what I wanted to do.

When I got home, I received an email alert that the studio director had been impressed enough to list me on the Internet Movie Database. IMDb is an online directory of actors, both movie and TV, as well as other players in the film industry. It's the most authoritative source for celebrity content, and to be listed after only a few shoots was a massive boost for me. It really lifted my spirits after the hell I had been living through with the loss of Dad.

I was now daring to believe that it could actually happen; that maybe I could make it in arguably one of the most unpredictable and elusive careers you could wish for. I had no illusions that movies and modelling, more often than not, is a world littered with broken dreams, but everything seemed to be heading in the right direction.

Now that I was on IMDb, I needed to raise my game to another level. The first thing I did was to upgrade my profile. I scrapped the selfies on my website and paid for specialised headshots. Within two weeks I had another assignment; another short film as a lead role with a lot of lines.

I still wasn't sure where all of this was taking me, but it certainly was going somewhere.

I did a few more film takes, getting more and more lines, and then suddenly got a call from an agency saying they would like to put me on their books to do an audition as an extra for a Paramount movie. They didn't tell me what the movie was or who was starring in it, but to me that didn't matter. Paramount is one of the biggest hitters in Hollywood.

It was to be a mass casting as they needed about 300 extras of all shapes and sizes to walk down streets, drink in pubs, and generally recreate life in London during the Second World War.

I arrived at the Gillette Studio and there were people milling about everywhere in a giant warehouse that was to be converted into the movie set. After reporting to the guy in charge of extras, I was hanging around waiting for instructions when someone came up and asked if I had done any feature stuff.

I had. He obviously thought I had the right look for a particular scene and gave me some lines to rehearse for an audition.

However, I needed to do the lines with a girl, so I looked around the seething crowd of extras to see who may be suitable.

One woman stood out. Not only was she pretty; she was the only one wearing a 1940s outfit that she had rented to look the part. I reckoned that as she was already conspicuous, the directors would notice me as well. She was definitely going the extra mile and I mentally gave her 10 out of 10 for initiative.

I walked up to her.

"Excuse me, would you mind helping me do my lines? It will really help me."

Fortunately, she didn't think this was some weird chat-up line, but even so, she was initially hesitant, saying she hadn't been asked to do an audition. She said she wasn't even an actress.

"That doesn't matter," I said. "I'm auditioning, so they'll notice you if you're with me when I read my lines."

That did the trick. She agreed, sold on the fact that this would also increase her profile.

We had about 10 minutes to pull it off. We read the lines and I thought I was probably pretty horrendous, seeing we had so little time to prepare. But the casting guy nodded as if he was happy.

I heard nothing further for about a month. Just as I thought I had been dropped, a woman from the agency called to say the movie people really liked me. She had another question; could I could sing? That floored me. Sure, I said, jokingly. I'm great in the shower.

She then told me Brad Pitt was to be the lead role in the movie.

Brad Pitt?

Yes, she replied. The movie was going to be called 'Allied'. It would, in all likelihood, be a massive blockbuster.

That took me even more by surprise than the question on whether I could sing. This was now a serious game changer with Brad Pitt in the movie. I wasn't going to miss out on it.

Of course I could sing, I said with as much conviction as I could muster.

She then asked me to pick any song from the 1940s and send her a demo file. I chose Vera Lynn's 'White Cliffs of Dover', as you can't get a more iconic English war song than that.

I then had to tape myself belting out a song I barely knew without any musical accompaniment. I emailed the file off, cringing inwardly, and braced myself for rejection.

Thirty minutes later I got a return email saying the agency liked my singing, and asked if I would do another Vera Lynn song, 'When the Lights go on Again'. This time I had a day to prepare.

Again, I was not over-optimistic with the end result. In fact, by now I was starting to suspect that I may be the brunt of one of those candid camera 'you've been framed' spoofs. I began to believe that someone was having me on for a joke.

But if it was true that Brad Pitt was involved in the movie, I was more than happy to risk being ridiculed.

To my surprise, I later got a call saying I had the singing part. I started practising right away as filming was scheduled in a few months' time.

I was later told that I would not have to sing the entire song alone, as the rest of the set would join in. They wanted me and another girl to sing the first couple of lines, and lead the others in.

Sadly, that didn't happen. The script writers in New York had to edit out 45 minutes, and my singing Vera Lynn was one of the casualties, ending up on the cutting room floor. Music will never be the same again!

So although I was only an extra, thanks to my singing audition I was one of the higher profile ones.

In one key take I was singled out and placed right next to Brad Pitt in a scene when he and Marion Cotillard, who played a French resistance fighter, announced their engagement.

Also starring was Jared Harris (son of Richard), so for much of the day I was in the company of A-listers. I then met Robert Zemeckis, who directed 'Forest Gump' and many other great films. That was a major 'wow' for me

I loved being on the set from the word go. The buzz, the vibe, the energy … everything pulsed with creative electricity. But I was astonished at how long it took to film a single act. The engagement scene with Brad and Marion must have been re-shot 40 times. I was told that was normal as Hollywood directors are fanatically meticulous. They're not just looking at the main stars; they're checking reflections in the window, or whether even the most obscure extras are facing in the right direction. If someone has moved slightly from their designated position, they'll re-do the scene. It's all put together in extreme detail.

In between takes, Brad, Jared and Marion mingled freely with us and were really friendly. If a shoot went well, Brad would smile, turn to us and say, "Good one."

My Game Valley background, where celebrities were treated the same as other visitors, came in handy on set and it was no big deal rubbing shoulders with A-listers. However, many of the extras were almost hyperventilating at times, whispering "My God, there's Brad Pitt!"

In the end, I was on set for two weeks, although I have to confess that I only appeared for about 12 seconds in the actual movie. Such is the life of an extra! I would have been seen a lot more if they hadn't cut my song, but even so, it was a fantastic experience. I now knew that this was exactly what I wanted to do. I knew where I was going.

My next break with an A-lister was with Liam Neeson in the suspense thriller, 'The Commuter'.

This was shot in Pinewood studios in Buckinghamshire, and like 'Allied' the script needed a lot of background actors. The set itself was intriguing; just a train coach with one side completely open enabling the cameras to zoom in and out while filming the action.

Once again, luck was on my side, just as it had been when I was selected to be next to Brad Pitt. This time the directors needed an extra to sit near Liam and told us to form up in a line so that they could make a selection. I got the part — or more correctly, the position, which guaranteed me camera exposure.

It may not sound like a big deal, but it is special for an extra to get noticed. Most are so far back in a scene that they're basically shadows or crowd clutter.

So there I was, waiting for the cameras to roll when Liam said, "Hey, I like your boots. Where did you get them?"

"I got them online." That, technically was true. What I didn't mention was that my mum had bought them for me as a gift.

He then asked where I was originally from and we spoke about Africa in detail. I told him that I would be returning soon after many years away.

"I'm also planning on making a short movie on where I grew up. On a game reserve in South Africa," I said.

He seemed genuinely interested in that and asked a few more questions before the cameras rolled.

I was surprised at his interest, which gave me an idea. If someone like Liam Neeson was interested in a mini-movie on growing up in Africa, maybe others would also be.

An idea started incubating in my mind. It was a small seed at first, but soon started sprouting.

I needed to revisit my roots. I needed to go back to Africa.

Chapter 20

Moving in the right direction

EETING BRAD PITT AND Liam Neeson may have been highlights, but those were bit roles that didn't pay the bills for long.

What was more important was that I was now starting to get noticed by directors in independent films. Everything was suddenly starting to happen. I was increasingly being offered meatier roles with far more lines.

The tempo was speeding up. Within two years of launching my acting career, I had worked on Transformers: The Last Knight; Torture; The Rizen and its sequel, The Rizen 2, where I play a scientist; Teenage Dream; Unreality;

301

My Best Friend's Wedding; Set Me Free; and 'Lee Reynold's Guide to Get Lucky', where I play the title character.

I was satisfied with the way things were going, as by any standards, that's not a bad list of roles coming my way in a relatively short period. The most gratifying aspect was seeing hard work starting to pay off. I found that I was not being invited to auditions to see if I can deliver; I was invited because I was expected to deliver.

Having said that, I've had some interesting auditions for roles I *didn't* get, such as one with Keanu Reeves in 'Siberia'. Unfortunately for me, the character I tested for was a 60-year-old guy, which meant the writers would have had to re-do the script to fit around someone who is half that age.

That's what I love about acting. If I fail, I do so on my own terms. Conversely, if I succeed, it's thanks to my personal sweat and toil. I live or die by my own decisions.

Failure is often a part of life in moments. For example, when I worked on Transformers as an extra, they did a close up of me where Director Michael Bay picked me out of the crowd with a very pretty female extra. It was a huge moment again for me to be selected by one of the best directors in the industry, and he was physically there filming us cheering for a goal scored in a Polo match. But when they did the final cut and the movie was released, they hardly used any of the three days filming they had done for that particular location and scene, so I wasn't seen. But there was a positive side to it; I had got that far to be chosen to be on set, then I was selected by the director himself for a close up in a huge film. You have to look for the positives and work on them to better yourself and strive higher. Failure is a form of growth and is sometimes destined to improve you, not hurt you.

In the U.K. we have an organization called Spotlight which is a member platform for actors, most of whom have studied in the arts or been to acting academies. I haven't done either, but due to building plenty of practical experience in a relatively short time I managed to get membership to this prestigious organization, which I consider to be a huge personal achievement. It's the equivalent of the Screen Actors Guild-American Federation of Television and Radio Artists (SAG-AFTRA) in Hollywood.

Also, movies and modelling is my first real individual achievement. I carved this career path totally on my own, whereas everything else just sort of happened for me. I was born into hotels, albeit deep in the bush, sent to hotel school, and slotted seamlessly into the hospitality industry. I enjoyed it immensely as I was very ambitious, but like my father I was always looking for something else. Some new challenge.

Then when I lost Dad, everything changed. It made me realise that I'm going to die one day as well. My youthful sense of immortality evaporated overnight. The only certainty is the uncertainty — you never know how much time you have on this planet. So it is more important doing something you love than it is doing something you have to.

Not everyone agrees with my new career choice. Some are saying I should focus on something more meaningful, or stick to what I know best, such as hotels. But to me my career is not just another job…it's much more personal. I'm feeling my way forward totally by myself. I'm following a path no one close to me has ever blazed. For me, one of the greatest kicks in life is knocking down walls that people say I can't.

Make no mistake, it was a substantial financial risk leaving the security of the hotel world to try and break into show business. Movies and modelling can be one of the most cut-throat games in town. You have to be a bit of a gambler to do it. My father always said you've got to risk it to get the biscuit — and he's absolutely right. I enjoy that philosophy much more now that I'm risking the biscuit for myself, not some corporate entity.

It's also true about my modelling career. I'm currently doing work at a much higher level. I've done shoots for iconic brands like Hugo Boss, Ralph Lauren and Tommy Hilfiger through El Corte Ingles in Spain. I've worked as well for Jacomo, GANT, Ben Sherman and Tesco, and have featured at the London Fashion Week, one of the Big Four clothing trade shows along with Paris, New York and Milan.

However, the best lesson I have learned is not how to be comfortable in front of cameras. Instead, it's how not to be scared of failure. If you are afraid of that, you will be paralysed from the start.

I learned this priceless lesson at my father's knee. He took massive risks and was prepared to live with the consequences. Coupled with that, he had huge stamina and perseverance. He just never gave up. The result was that he rarely failed.

This was true also of Carolyn Boyd, my guardian who played a pivotal part in my life. Her influence on me cannot be overstated. She always encouraged me to follow my dreams, whether I was considering going to Jamaica or for a movie audition. It is no small thanks to her that today I am living the dream. Carolyn showed me that you stand out if you don't stand back — without, of course, being rude or annoying.

This advice has stood me in good stead, no matter what I have done. As a young hotel director, I could walk into a room of high-flying corporate bankers and instinctively knew how to present myself. In the movie industry, I had the confidence to regard A-listers as just ordinary people with extraordinary talent, rather than superstars or superior beings.

For example, I once bumped into Meryl Steep. I was in Los Angeles about a year after Dad had died and was browsing in a store called Whole Foods, when I noticed her in one of the aisles. She had been one of Dad's most revered actresses, and as earlier mentioned, 'Out of Africa' was his all-time favourite film. He watched it numerous times.

She was on her own and I immediately thought of Dad. I only had one chance to do this, so I walked up to her and told her how much 'Out of Africa' had meant to my father. Essentially, I thanked her for giving him so much happiness and how he had lived an adventurous life similar to the characters in the film. At the same time, I was respectful of her privacy and apologised for interrupting her.

She was gracious and kind said she was sorry for my loss. I think it was also rather refreshing for her not to be mobbed for a selfie or autograph, but instead hear what her exceptional talent actually meant to her fans. My dad had touched so many people's lives, so it was special for me to actually thank someone who had touched his, even if it had been so vicariously.

That meeting also sparked rich memories for me. I too was 'Out of Africa', something I had been blessed with through luck and circumstance. I owed everything to my upbringing. There is no doubt in my mind that I have persisted and thrived in a tough industry because I have managed to reap what I learned from the bush and my father's wonderful wisdom.

Like wild animals, you meet some vicious people in the movie world and you have to know how to handle them. You have to evaluate your environment and handle it correctly to survive in both real and concrete jungles. You have to develop a strong shell. The circle of life and death is all around you, and once you are able to accept that in the wild, you accept it anywhere. In other words, the bush teaches you not to sweat the small stuff.

I was fortunate to have a foot in two worlds; both as a child of the outdoors and simultaneously learning social urban skills. But as I started to get older, and perhaps a little wiser, I began to realise just how deep my personal debt to Africa was.

Everything I had done, successful or otherwise, is thanks to my native continent.

The time had come to go back.

Chapter 21

Returning home a boy

I DON'T ROMANTICISE AFRICA. Despite its beauty, both physical and spiritual, it can also be a place of much hardship.

I was lucky and privileged to have lived a good life there, something I am intensely aware of. My experiences are not everyday ones. The life I lived is different from most South Africans.

But even though we were cocooned by our piece of paradise at Karkloof, our family has experienced violence first hand. My mother has been mugged twice, once quite viciously in Pietermaritzburg, where she screamed so loudly that the robber dropped her handbag. The second time was equally harrowing on a trip to Cape Town after my father died. She was wearing a pendant of Africa, given to her by Dad and consequently of incalculable sentimental value. It was ripped off her neck when she was attacked by eight youths.

She reported the matter to the police and a constable taking her statement demanded she prove she was from England by producing pound notes. She pulled £10 out of her purse, which he promptly grabbed. He then asked if she had anymore, which he took as well. Fortunately, another cop arrived and the officer quickly handed the notes back, asking why she had 'given' them to him.

Mum's experiences are mild compared to most of the victims of the rocketing crime rate in the country. But even so, the good in South Africa still far, far outweighs the horror. It always will.

I returned to the land of my birth when I was 32. It had been 16 years since I had last set foot on African soil, and before I caught the plane, I had some serious misgiving about coming back after all those years. My father's key philosophy had always been to look forward, not back. In the final days before his death, we spoke about Africa and our memories are magnificent. But both of us had moved on.

However, just as Dad went back to retire in Devon, where he grew up as a young boy, I was increasingly feeling a magnetic pull to return to my boyhood home.

I also wanted to return as a 'boy'. In other words, with the same sense of awe, wonder, freedom and excitement that I had grown up with. Not only that, as I had told Liam Neeson, I wanted to make a short film about it. I would call it 'Returning Home a Boy' for that very reason. It would be a personal odyssey, coming to terms with my past and confronting my future. In other words, returning to my boyhood home as a man, but through the eyes of a boy.

As we landed at O.R. Tambo airport in Johannesburg, the blood bond I had forged with the land as a child came back so viscerally that I thought I would choke. It was a primeval and powerful sensation. Although Africa is no longer my geographical home, it is still a spiritual one.

With me were two friends who would be my media team; Director of Photography Tom Baker and Dr John Jones, my Brand Manager at the time. I met John soon after Dad died and we formed an instant connection as his father had recently died as well. We play loads of squash together and he has been a massive help helping me get ahead in the movie industry. He said I had the necessary attributes, but his key message was I would regret more not doing it and saying 'what if', than I ever would trying and failing. It was so true — not just about movies, but about life.

Tom and I had done some work previously together and I discovered right away that he's very good at what he does.

From Johannesburg we took a connecting flight to Pietermaritzburg and my excitement grew. Then as we arrived at Karkloof, approaching the gate to Game Valley, it was as though someone from above had arranged a special welcoming committee.

If I hadn't seen it, I would never have believed it. For there, at the majestic stone-and-thatch entrance, were scores of animals. There were rhinos, nyala, zebra, impala, buffaloes, giraffe, warthogs … you name it. Just about every species of mammal you find on the reserve had pitched up.

Obviously, they hadn't come to say 'welcome home' to me. But I am sentimental, so you will forgive me for thinking otherwise. It was the most fantastic homecoming I could imagine, let alone hope for.

I bowed my head. I then knelt and kissed the earth. My tears spilled onto the ground, soaked up by the soil. It was the same soil that holds my first footprints.

I sensed my father's hand on my shoulder. This — spread out gloriously before me — was his vision. It was still alive, with such splendid richness that I almost had to pinch myself. I knew Dad was there.

As we drove in, I felt like a long-lost son returning from epic wanderings on another planet. This was my first home; a home that had nurtured who I was. A home that in one way or another influenced everything I did.

As we drove to the lodge, I remembered every bump on the road; nothing seemed to have changed. It was like meeting a friend after many years and resuming a conversation as if it was yesterday.

We passed the waterfall and I told Tom and John that this wasn't just a picture-postcard scene; this was the valley's aorta — it's beating heart. The forests, the fertile land, the people and the animals thrive thanks to this exuberant tumbling spray of water.

I pointed out where we had done helter-skelter game captures for buffalo, where I had almost been run over by a rampaging troop of razor-tusked warthogs. I showed them where we had dived into the river from boulders the size of double storey buildings; where Mum had jumped over a puff adder during her morning jog; where Pugga and I had fled a wildebeest and its calf. I even showed them where I had my first toke, unknowingly, of marijuana when I was just five.

I pointed out where Big Boy had charged Dad, Jamie and me as we sped off on the three-wheeler with seconds to spare. Where Big Boy had gored Doug. This story became even more real for them when we walked into the lodge hallway and Big Boy's enormous skull was on display. He died of old age several years ago, and my eyes dampened as I looked at the relic of my old friend. He was the Mike Tyson of the rhino world and a celebrity in his own right. People came from all around the world to see him.

He and I had grown up together. I raised my hand in a salute and whispered 'well done brother' with absolute love and respect for an indomitable character.

The new owner, Fred Wörner, told us that he too had a close call with Big Boy. There had been some noise near his room one night and he went outside to investigate. He tripped on the patio stairs and suddenly a bulk came out of the blackness, fast as a bullet.

At the last moment, for some reason, Big Boy veered off. Maybe it was because Fred had fallen to the ground, which is what you are advised to do if there are no trees to climb during a rhino charge. But it was a near thing.

Just pointing to that enormous horn the size of a cutlass told the story for Tom and John more intensely than I could have.

Fred Wörner has ploughed a considerable amount of money into the reserve. It's now called the Karkloof Safari Spa and boasts a hugely prestigious Seven Stars and Stripes Award, the only game reserve to have won such award on the entire continent of Africa.

Fred has done a superb job at Karkloof. It's a lot more upmarket than it was when Mum and Dad ran it, but the conservation ethos is still very much in evidence. The animals are thriving and multiplying — so much so that Fred has had to buy a neighbouring farm to accommodate the burgeoning population. From a Meyer point of view, we could not have sold Game Valley to a better guy. The soul, the spirit and ethos of this magnificent patch of Africa is flourishing.

Co-incidentally, one of the guests when we arrived was head of National Geographic in India, a major player in the conservation world. He was intrigued when he heard that I was the son of the guy who had created the reserve and the deep spiritual connection I had with it.

Seeing his interest, I opened up. I told him the story of the Valley of Heaven and how my dad had carved it out of overgrown bush used to graze semi-feral cattle into a world class wilderness. Wilderness is by definition untouched, but the reality is that Game Valley was designated farmland before Dad arrived. The Eden before us was purely his vision. Without him, we would be looking at crops and cows.

I pointed to the hills that had been rebuilt with bulldozers and Earth Movers after the disastrous floods of 1987. I told him about Thembi the orphaned elephant calf, who played in our back garden while city kids played with puppies and kittens. I told him about riding elephants in the bush with Doug Groves; about jumping on Big Boy's back thinking he was a slab of stone; about being bitten by snakes.

He was blown away with the story of what this place had meant to so many people.

Later, after doing a video session with Tom, I saw, a warthog — possibly one of Maggie's grandchildren — and her baby nearby. I filmed the two of them on my iPhone when suddenly the mama charged. I just managed to get out of her way and we put the clip on Youtube. In half an hour we had got more than 5,000 views.

That set me off thinking. Tom, John and I had started filming the travelogue about me 'returning home a boy' while also doing a top-quality commercial for Fred and the Safari Spa. But in only one week of experimenting, we had picked up thousands of social media followers. In fact, we were getting so much attention that I thought maybe we were onto something. Maybe we were missing a trick by not taking it further.

Instead of shooting a short video and a promo for the wonderful work that Fred is now doing, why not do a full documentary? Not just as a travel piece, but as a tribute to Dad who was without question a conservation visionary? Could this trip be bigger than nostalgic musings of a son returning to his boyhood home after losing a much-loved father?

I always back myself whenever I get an idea, and if I fail, I fail epically. But if I succeed, it can be equally epic. There are no half-measures. Either I push through with a project accepting the possibility of regretting it, or I end up regretting that I never pushed through. I always go ahead and live with the consequences. I back myself because the consequences have usually been good.

John and Tom were crucial for this to work, even though we hadn't initially come out to Africa for anything epic. I initially brought John along to handle the website work while I did the story. Tom was a great cameraman whom I had done shoots with before and I loved his work. Now I was asking them to consider doing a much bigger project.

They were both up for it. In fact, both separately told me how powerful the all-embracing ambience of Game Valley was for them. It was an ectoplasm of ancient Africa; a wilderness time capsule, although the lodge and luxury spa were certainly 21st Century. But it was the wilderness we were interested in. That, not the man-made structures on Karkloof, is what had succoured me as a child.

I decided to take them to the top of a remote hill on the far side of the valley looking back to the lodge. It was where Dad and I often chatted. For me, this was a sacred place. It was a cathedral of the bush where Dad had said so many wonderful things, most of which I only grasped as I grew.

It was a beautiful evening, the sun setting in vivid shades of red, ranging from blood to salmon pink. I poured them a drink and handed out some biltong, dried meat, either game or beef, that is an iconic African food.

The sun dipped below the horizon. We brought out chairs and I said, "Close your eyes and put your head back."

They did as I said.

"Okay, now open your eyes and see the blanket of the sky and soak up the glory of wild Africa."

My words were not poetic, but they got it right away. The magic of wild places is all around you in Karkloof. That's true poetry.

Although so much blood has been spilt by both man and beast, there is still that wonderful essence of Africa that is surreally virginal. It's an ancient land, the birthplace of humanity, but yet everything seems new and fresh. Whether you are an African or not, it still gets to you. The land is an intense assault of the senses — the smell, the sun, the dust, the sky, the animals. You will never see or sense that unique primal splendour anywhere else.

Tom and John understood. It was a defining moment as the sun faded to dusk then night, gloriously ignited by countless stars in the megawatt sky. Both told me afterwards the trip had changed their lives.

I could visualise my father smiling. That was exactly what his vision had been. To change lives.

That's what was so majestic about this trip. Dad's dream was intrinsically still so alive. Karkloof was buzzing with vibrancy. The lodge itself may be a luxury spa, but the unchanged wilderness was eternally out there, raw and gorgeous. The animals were safe with the steep cliffs and kopjes as natural sentinels. There was no poaching. The buffalo herd was still disease-free.

I now understood with absolute clarity what Dad's amazing vision had been all along. When he bought Game Valley, many people said he was crazy. He had already made millions; why would he spend his fortune on something like this? Something so fickle, so ethereal, and with no guarantee of financial reward? An investment that could so easily go south?

He did it because he loved it, and also because he could see deeper into the ether beyond than most. He could see that what he had created would not only survive, but flourish. And that's exactly what happened.

This had initially been a trip about closure; returning home a boy. About closing the African chapter once and for all, but also celebrating the fact that under Fred Wörner, the reserve is still thriving.

It had morphed into much more than that. It was now about opening new doors. I saw how I could bring this whole odyssey back to life.

I have never truly told people about my background and childhood in case I came across as arrogant, and my dad's scorn for arrogance was immeasurable. I didn't want to say, hey, I grew up as in a safari park and had an elephant as a pet. Hey, I survived snake bites and rhino charges.

It was a story I didn't even know I wanted to tell.

But when you whittle it down to the marrow, distill the words in acid, the story is simple. It's about dreams and striving to make them come true. About living life on your own terms, facing fears, facing failures and accepting success with humility.

I have been bequeathed a precious gift. I was shown by a maestro that living the dream, from Africa to wherever you choose, is a moveable feast.

You can take it wherever you want. Otherwise you will lose it.

Dreams only come true if you have the guts to pursue them. That, for me, is the lesson of my father.

If you don't follow your dreams, you only have yourself to blame.

The End

<u>Dedications</u>

Dad

I miss you dearly Dad and as Les put it, I know you are re-creating Heaven to be even greater for us later. I am who I am, thanks to so much of your love, your wisdom, your guidance, and your forgiveness with constant patience. You allowed to me to fly by not just giving me wings but by creating the wind to lift me even higher. You allowed me to not just have footsteps but to leave lasting footprints. Every day I look in the mirror and I see you. I treasure you, I treasure your legacy and I treasure the responsibility to live life by the lessons and manners you taught me. I will try passing them to others and my children one day. I hope this book does you justice, and that in some way these words float in the winds and get carried by the angels to you with my love and affection. I'll listen for your echo in the wind and I'll see you in my dreams. Don't rest in peace, rest now living how you always did with fun, adventure, charm, charisma and wings to fly even further to your next destiny. You are always my hero.

Mum

From the beginning you have been constant love and support. I wouldn't be following my dreams today if I hadn't had you there by my side. I know how challenging it has been for you after losing dad but he would be so proud of you and the strength you developed. You are an incredible mother and friend. Life has knocked you down many times and you have the grit and determination to keep fighting on. I have learned so much from you and know our bond is even stronger after Dad. Many mothers should look to you for good advice and guidance as you are the perfect example of a special mother. I am so lucky to have been blessed with you as my mum. Thank you for being you.

My Guardian

Carolyn you have been such an important and amazing part of my life. I wouldn't be where I am without your guidance along the way. You taught me so much and supported me even more. Your greatest gift to me was, and still is, giving me the confidence to use my wings and go get it in all my crazy adventures. Even when I couldn't see it properly you would help open my eyes. From swimming in a river with you to living abroad on my own you helped me overcome anything. You are constantly so loving and I can't thank you enough for being the incredible person you are. You have always been like a mum to me.

Tony & Julia Röbin

Ever since I came to the UK as a, bigger than usual, 10 yr old boy, you have been there throughout as inspiring people in my life. You created my best friend Charlie and have accepted me into your family as #2 son. You are the coolest of parents by far with the epic parties and best wines that never run dry. But you have always been there for me and supported me. Any major event in my life, you were there celebrating and even my hardest moment, with losing Dad, you were there to hold me up and push me forward. I can't thank you enough for you love, support and constant laughter. Tony, you really have been the Big Daddy.

Friends & Influencers

Thank you to all my friends who have supported me throughout and influenced the better side of my life. You mean a lot to me and I hope this book encourages any of you to keep striving. Especially my Les Roches friends who helped create my "way of life", I am grateful for you all as we were such a family on that Rock. To all the people who helped create my opportunities and the agents who believed in me, thank you. Your belief and trust has given me the confidence to go higher. But, to my Best Friend Charlie Robin, thank you for always being there, little brother, as you have been such a huge part of my life for so many years. I am grateful that we have shared so much and know you and I are like Dad and Deneys.

Graham Spence – My Ghost-writer and friend

Huge special thanks must go to you Graham. Without you this book was never going to be possible. After reading "The Elephant Whisperer" there was no doubt you were the only person to write this. You write with passion and you inspire as you tell it from the heart. I had to wait 6 months for you before we could start this journey together, but it was worth the wait. This year with you has brought so much back to life, for many of us. Your patience was appreciated and your gift to write in ways I never could has been incredible. You have brought soul, character and humour to this project. I am grateful for our friendship and hope we stay close for many more years to come. Thank you eternally Graham.

Other books by Graham

The Lawrence Anthony Trilogy

Babylon's Ark

The Elephant Whisperer

The Last Rhinos

Chris Stone Trilogy

The Apocalypse Chase

Bloodhorn

Bloodbelief *(still to be released)*

(www.grahamspence.com)

Printed in Great Britain
by Amazon